The
iPod

How to do just the useful and fun
stuff with your iPod and iTunes **Book**

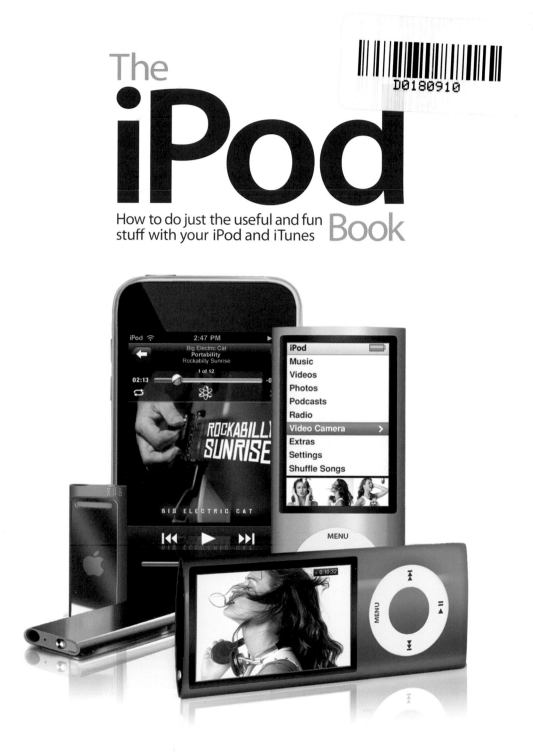

iPod 2:47 PM

Big Electric Cat
Portability
Rockabilly Sunrise

1 of 12

02:13

ROCKABILLY
SUNRISE

BIG ELECTRIC CAT

| iPod |
| Music |
| Videos |
| Photos |
| Podcasts |
| Radio |
| Video Camera |
| Extras |
| Settings |
| Shuffle Songs |

MENU

MENU

Scott Kelby

The iPod Book, Sixth Edition

The iPod Book Team

CREATIVE DIRECTOR
Felix Nelson

TRAFFIC DIRECTOR
Kim Gabriel

PRODUCTION MANAGER
Dave Damstra

TECHNICAL EDITORS
Kim Doty
Cindy Snyder
Terry White

DESIGNER
Jessica Maldonado

STUDIO SHOTS
Scott Kelby

PUBLISHED BY
Peachpit Press

Copyright © 2010 by Scott Kelby

FIRST PRINTING: November 2009

Composed in Myriad, Lucida Grande, and Helvetica by Kelby Publishing.

Trademarks
All terms mentioned in this book that are known to be trademarks or service marks have been appropriately capitalized. Peachpit Press cannot attest to the accuracy of this information. Use of a term in the book should not be regarded as affecting the validity of any trademark or service mark.

iPod, iTunes, Macintosh, and Mac are registered trademarks of Apple Inc.
Windows is a registered trademark of Microsoft Corporation.
Photoshop Elements is a registered trademark of Adobe Systems, Inc.

Warning and Disclaimer
This book is designed to provide information about iPods. Every effort has been made to make this book as complete and as accurate as possible, but no warranty of fitness is implied.

The information is provided on an as-is basis. The author and Peachpit Press shall have neither liability nor responsibility to any person or entity with respect to any loss or damages arising from the information contained in this book or from the use of the discs or programs that may accompany it.

ISBN 13: 978-0-321-64906-5
ISBN 10:   0-321-64906-0
9 8 7 6 5 4 3 2 1

Printed and bound in the United States of America

For my wonderfully talented book designer,
Jessica Maldonado. One of the best things
that ever happened to my books is you!

Acknowledgments

Although only one name appears on this book's spine, it takes a large, dedicated team of people to put a book like this together. Not only did I have the good fortune of working with such a great group of people, I now get the great pleasure of thanking them and acknowledging their hard work and dedication.

First, I'd like to thank my wonderful, amazing, hilarious, fun-filled, and loving wife, Kalebra. You're part wonder woman, part supermom, part business exec, part rock star, and part standup comic, and every day you manage to put a smile on my lips and a song in my heart. Your spirit, warmth, beauty, patience, and unconditional love continue to prove what everybody always says—I'm the luckiest guy in the world. Thank you for saying "Yes" 20 years ago this year!

I also want to thank my nearly 13-year-old son, Jordan. I'm so proud of him, so thrilled to be his dad, and I love watching him turn into the wonderful "little man" he has become. He has so many of his mother's special gifts, especially her boundless heart, and it's amazing the amount of joy he brings into my life.

Also, the single best thing that can happen to a person happened to me—God blessed our family with the birth of an adorable, happy, healthy little baby girl—Kira Nicole Kelby. She's 3¹/₂ now and she's a little clone of her mother, which is about the best thing that could happen to her.

Thanks to my big brother Jeff for all the wonderful things you've done for me (and for other people) and for having so much of our dad in you. Your humor, generosity, and compassion are an inspiration. I love you, man.

For this edition of the book (the sixth edition), I asked my good friend, and co-author of *The iPhone Book,* to be the book's technical editor, and take all the techniques through their paces. If there's anybody who knows more about the iPod and iTunes, I've yet to meet him, and that's why I had to ask Terry White to tech edit this book for me, and it's a far better book because of his input, ideas, and contributions. Thanks man—you rock!

A big thanks to my in-house editor Kim Doty, who is just about to be a mommy for the second time (in fact, by the time you read this, she'll be cuddling a sweet little baby girl). It is both an absolute pleasure, and an honor, to get to work with you on these books. Also, thanks to Cindy Snyder for all your hard work, help, and ideas in making this, and all my books, a reality.

Thanks to my brilliant Creative Director, Felix Nelson, for rallying the troops as only he can, and for taking me to Ocean Prime for actually getting my writing done on schedule.

To my best buddy and book-publishing powerhouse, Dave Moser (also known as "the guiding light, force of nature, miracle birth, etc."), for always insisting that we raise the bar and make everything we do better than anything we've done before.

Much love to my amazing creative team at Kelby Media Group (folks like Jessica Maldonado, who comes up with all the cool interior and cover designs, and Dave Damstra): I simply couldn't do it without you, and it's a pleasure to be a part of such an amazingly creative group of individuals.

I couldn't do any of this without the help and support of my wonderful assistant, Kathy Siler, without whom I'd be sitting in my office mumbling and staring at the ceiling. She's my right-hand-man (even though she's a woman) and makes my work life have order, calm, and sense. She is the best.

Thanks to my good friend, Jean A. Kendra, for her support and enthusiasm for all my writing projects, and for being such a great friend to our family.

Thanks to my friends at Peachpit Press, especially my Editor (and generally cool guy) Ted Waitt, my publisher Nancy Aldrich-Ruenzel, to Scott Cowlin, Sara Jane Todd, and the whole crew at Peachpit who make writing books an awful lot of fun, which is very rare in this industry.

Thanks to my mentors whose wisdom and whip-cracking have helped me immeasurably throughout my life, including John Graden, Jack Lee, Dave Gales, Judy Farmer, and Douglas Poole.

A personal thanks to my buddies Jeff Revell, Marvin Derezin, Rod Harlan, Mike Kubeisy, Dave Cross, Matt Kloskowski, Dave Cuerdon, Corey Barker, RC, Terry White, Larry Becker, Vanelli, and Felix, just for being my buddies.

Thanks to the whole team at Kelby Media Group, for their commitment to excellence, for refusing to accept limitations, and for being an example of what's best about this industry.

And most importantly, an extra special thanks to God and His son Jesus Christ for always hearing my prayers, for always being there when I need Him, and for blessing me with such a wonderful life, and such a warm, loving family to share it with.

About the Author

Scott Kelby

Scott is Editor-in-Chief and Publisher of *Photoshop User* magazine, and Editor-in-Chief and Publisher of *Layers* magazine. He is President and co-founder of the National Association of Photoshop Professionals (NAPP), the trade association for Adobe® Photoshop® users, and President of the software, education, and publishing firm Kelby Media Group.

Scott is a photographer, designer, and award-winning author of more than 50 books on technology and digital imaging, including the best-selling books: *The iPhone Book*, *The Digital Photography Book*, volumes 1, 2, and 3, and *The Photoshop Book for Digital Photographers*. Scott has authored several best-selling Macintosh books, including the award-winning *Macintosh: The Naked Truth*, from New Riders, and *The Mac OS X Leopard Book* and *Mac OS X Leopard Killer Tips* from Peachpit Press. His books have been translated into dozens of different languages, including Russian, Chinese, French, German, Spanish, Korean, Greek, Turkish, Japanese, Dutch, and Taiwanese, among others.

For the past five years straight, Scott has been awarded the distinction of being the world's No. 1 best-selling author of all computer and technology books, across all categories. His book, *The Digital Photography Book*, volume 1, is the best-selling book on digital photography of all time.

Scott is Training Director for the Adobe Photoshop Seminar Tour, Conference Technical Chair for the Photoshop World Conference & Expo, and is a speaker at trade shows and events around the world. For more information on Scott, visit his daily blog at www.scottkelby.com.

CHAPTER ONE   1

Start Me Up
Learning That Essential Stuff

Charging Your Battery (Using the USB Cable) 2
Where iTunes Fits In 3
Importing Songs from a CD 4
Importing Songs Already on Your Computer 5
Downloading Songs from the iTunes Store 6
Creating a Playlist 7
Getting Music onto Your iPod 8
Getting Your New Songs onto Your iPod 9
Using Your iPod nano or iPod classic 10
Playing Songs, Volume, and Stuff Like That 11
Playing Video on Your iPod 12
Done Listening? Put It to Sleep 13
Turning On the Backlight 14
Controlling Your Screen's Brightness 15
How's Your Battery Life? 16
Replacing Your iPod's Battery 17

CHAPTER TWO   19

Nano-Nucleonic Cyborg Summoning
Using Your iPod nano or classic

Customizing the Main Menu 20
Searching for Songs Made Easy 21
Visual Searching with Cover Flow 22
Shuffling Your Song Order 23
Shake Your nano to Turn on Shuffle 24
Repeating the Current Song or Playlist 25
Rating Your Favorites 26
Creating a Playlist Right on
Your iPod (On-The-Go) 27
Make a Genius Playlist on Your iPod 28
Enhancing Your Sound Quality (EQ) 29
Saving Your Ears from Volume Abuse 30
Finding Out How Much Space Is Left
for More Songs and Videos 31
Deleting a Song from Your iPod 32
Listening to Audiobooks on Your iPod 33
Setting an Alarm 34
Your iPod Has Three Built-In Games 35
Creating Voice Memos on Your iPod nano 36
Listening to Your iPod nano's FM Radio 37

Table of Contents

Pausing Live FM Radio on Your iPod nano 38
Exercising with Your iPod nano. 39
Getting Your iPod nano to Talk to You 40

CHAPTER THREE   **43**

It's Tricky
Cool iPod Tips & Tricks

Using Your iPod as a Removable Hard Disk 44
Stopping Your iPod from Syncing Every Time. 45
Troubleshooting: Your iPod Won't Turn On. 46
What to Do If Your iPod Locks Up. 47
Use Your iPod as a Contact Manager 48
Safeguard Your iPod with Screen Lock. 49
A Playlist Just on Your iPod but Not in iTunes 50

CHAPTER FOUR   **53**

Video Killed the Radio Star
Video on Your iPod nano or classic

Buying and Renting Movies from the
iTunes Store 54
Downloading TV Shows from the iTunes Store 55
A Faster Way to Find Videos in the Store 56
Getting Videos onto Your iPod 57
Getting Home Movies to Play on Your iPod 58
Watching iPod Videos on Your TV 59
Video Podcasts Aren't Under Videos on
Your iPod 60
Moving Your Movies to Another Computer. 61
Shooting Video on Your iPod nano 62
Adding Effects to Your Videos on Your iPod nano 63
Transferring Your iPod nano Videos to
Your Computer 64

CHAPTER FIVE   **67**

Get the Freeze-Frame
Using Your iPod's Photo Features

Mac: Getting Photos on Your iPod. 68
Windows PC: Getting Photos on Your iPod 69
Viewing Photos You've Imported. 70
Seeing a Slide Show of Your Photos 71
Customizing Your Slide Show 72
Seeing Your Slide Show on TV. 73
Getting Your Stored Photos
onto Your Computer. 74

CHAPTER SIX   **77**

iTouch Myself

Using Your iPod touch

Turning Your iPod touch On and Off 78

Using the Home Screen 79

Rearranging Your Home Screen Icons 80

What Double-Clicking the
Home Button Does 81

Playing a Song 82

Scrubbing, Repeating, and Shuffling 83

Seeing the Other Songs on an Album 84

Getting to Your Playlists 85

Making On-The-Go Playlists 86

Creating Genius Playlists 87

Using the Automatic Genius Mix 88

Searching for Songs Already on Your iPod 89

Visual Searching by Album Cover 90

Controlling Your iPod While in
Another App 91

Changing the Buttons at the
Bottom of the Music App 92

Finding Stuff in the iTunes Store 93

Downloading Audio and Video Podcasts 94

Watching Videos 95

Deleting Videos 96

Renting Movies 97

Connect Your iPod touch
to Your TV 98

Downloading Apps 99

Deleting Apps 100

Getting New Features and
Bug Fixes for Apps 101

Using the Built-In Keyboard 102

Getting a Much Larger Keyboard 103

Copying-and-Pasting Stuff 104

Getting Internet Access 105

Using the Safari Web Browser 106

Using the Built-In Google Search 107

Working with Multiple Webpages 108

Importing Bookmarks from Your Computer 109

Completing Online Forms 110

Watching YouTube Videos 111

Syncing Your Calendar 112

Syncing Your Contacts 113

Adding an Email Account 114
Checking Your Email 115
Reading Your Email 116
How to Email a Photo 117
Make a Photo Your Startup Wallpaper 118
Using Maps to Find Just About Anything 119
Finding Your Contacts on the Map 120
Getting Driving Directions 121
Drop a Pin on the Map 122
Display More Information on the Map 123
Use Map Bookmarks 124
Seeing Your Local Weather 125
Using the Calculator 126
Getting Stock Quotes 127
Making Quick Notes 128
Have Your iPod Sing You to Sleep 129
Using the Other Clock Features 130
Using the Stopwatch 131
Using Voice Control to Control
Your iPod touch 132
Using the Built-in Voice Memos App 133
Using a Wireless Bluetooth Headset 134
Using the Nike + iPod Sport Kit for Runners 135

CHAPTER SEVEN   137
Home Sweet Home
iTunes Essentials
See Just the Info You Want 138
Finding a Particular Song 139
Editing Your Song's Info 140
Adding Song Lyrics 141
Use Browsing to Create Instant Playlists 142
Deleting Songs in a Playlist (Two Things
You Need to Know) 143
Burning a CD of Songs 144
Setting the Gap Between Burned Songs 145
Set Up Your CDs to Import Automatically 146
Auto-Naming for Imported CD Songs 147
Combining Two Tracks into One 148
Playing Live Albums Without Pauses
Between Songs 149
How Much Free Space Is Left on Your iPod 150
Organizing the Songs on Your Hard Disk 151

CHAPTER EIGHT   **153**
Imaginary Player
Working with Playlists

Putting Your Songs in Your Order 154
Deleting Songs (and Playlists). 155
Rearranging Your Column Order 156
Combining Two Playlists into One. 157
How Rating Your Songs Helps. 158
Have iTunes Make Smart Playlists
for You 159
A Smart Playlist Idea for Short Trips. 160
Cutting Clutter with Playlist Folders 161
Create a Genius Playlist in iTunes. 162
Let Genius Find Songs You
Don't Own (Yet) 163
Genius Mixes Do All the Work for You 164
Using iTunes as Your Party DJ 165
Letting Your Party Guests Control
the Music. 166

CHAPTER NINE   **169**
Proof of Purchase
Using the iTunes Store

Getting Around the iTunes Store 170
Finding Stuff in the iTunes Store 171
You Can Browse in the iTunes Store, Too! 172
A Source for Musical Inspiration 173
Can't Find It? Try a Power Search 174
The Shortcut from iTunes to the iTunes Store 175
Buying Songs or Adding Them to
Your Wish List. 176
Upgrading Your Old Songs to Be
DRM-Free 177
Allowing Multiple Simultaneous Downloads 178
Why You Need to Back Up What You Buy 179
Keeping an Eye on Your Spending 180
Protect Yourself from Getting Ripped Off. 181
Setting Up an iTunes Allowance. 182
Keeping Naughty Videos from the Kids. 183
Telling Your Friends About Cool Albums. 184
Spreading the Word on Facebook and Twitter 185
Letting Other People Listen to Your Music. 186
Sharing Your Stuff with Family 187
Speeding Up Sharing and Previews 188

A Real Album Experience with
iTunes LPs 189

Getting Movie Bonus Content
(Like You Do on DVDs) 190

Moving Your Purchases to
Another Computer 191

CHAPTER TEN   **193**

Tip Drill

Cool iTunes Tips & Tricks

Browse Your Music in Cover Flow View 194

Browse Your Music in Grid View 195

Making Sure All Your Songs Are Rated.............. 196

Adding Smooth Transitions Between Songs 197

Balancing the Volume Between Songs 198

Making Your Music Sound Better.................... 199

Individual EQ Settings by Song 200

Editing a Song's Start/End Points................... 201

How Many Playlists Does a Song
Appear In?... 202

Moving Playlists Between Computers 203

Finding Your Originals for Easy Backup 204

Printing Your Own CD Jewel Case Inserts........... 205

Printing Song and Album Listings.................. 206

iTunes Radio Is on the Air!......................... 207

It's Time to Get Visual 208

Extreme Visuals................................... 209

CHAPTER ELEVEN   **211**

Lido Shuffle

Using Your iPod shuffle

Automatically Getting Songs onto
Your iPod shuffle................................... 212

Manually Adding Songs to Your
iPod shuffle.. 213

The Stuff on Top of Your iPod shuffle 214

Playing Music on Your iPod shuffle 215

Checking Your Battery Life 216

Getting Your shuffle to Talk to You................. 217

Storing Other Files on Your iPod shuffle 218

INDEX 219

Seven Things You'll Wish You Had Known...

SCOTT KELBY

(1) The first chapter is for people brand new to the iPod (you just opened the box), so if you've had your iPod for a few months now and you already know how to turn it on, how to play a song, put it to sleep, etc., you can skip right over to Chapter 2 and start there. It won't hurt my feelings one bit (but you might want to at least skim through Chapter 1 anyway. Hey, ya never know).

(2) You don't have to read it chapter by chapter. Outside of that first I-just-opened-the-box chapter, I designed this to be a "jump-in-anywhere" book. You don't have to read it in order, chapter by chapter—if you want to learn how to do a certain thing, just find it in the Table of Contents, turn to that page, and you'll have the answer in seconds. Each page shows you how to do just one important thing. One topic. One idea. For example, if you want to learn how to read an email on your iPod touch, I'll show you, step by step, how to do exactly that.

(3) I didn't totally "geek out." I wrote everything just as if a friend came over to my house, pulled out their new iPod, and started asking me questions. So, for example, if you were at my house and you turned to me and said, "Hey Scott, is there a way to see more of this webpage on my iPod touch's screen?" I wouldn't go into how the touch's built-in vibrotactile actuator works. In real life, I'd turn to you and say, "Just turn it sideways and it switches to a wider view." I'd tell you short, sweet, and right to the point, just like that. So that's what I do throughout the book. It's not a "tell-me-all-about-it" book; instead it's a "show-me-how-to-do-it" book.

(4) How to know which parts are for you: The iTunes stuff mostly applies to everybody— no matter which iPod you have—but since the iPod touch has such different controls and features, it has its own separate chapter (Chapter 6), and so does the iPod shuffle

Before Reading This Book!

SCOTT KELBY

(Chapter 11). The controls for the iPod nano are pretty much identical to the iPod classic's controls, so they're both covered in the same chapters (where there's a difference, I let you know. For example, the iPod nano has a built-in video camera, but the iPod classic doesn't, so the heading for that page is "Shooting Video on Your iPod nano." If I don't call out a particular iPod (nano or classic) in the header—it's for both. Don't forget, though, no matter which iPod you have (touch, nano, classic, or shuffle), you'll be using iTunes to manage your music, so make sure you read those chapters, too.

(5) The intro page at the beginning of each chapter is designed to give you a quick mental break, and honestly, they have little to do with the chapter. In fact, they have little to do with anything, but writing these off-the-wall chapter intros is kind of a tradition of mine (I do this in all my books), but if you're one of those really "serious" types, you can skip them because they'll just get on your nerves.

(6) Look at the bottom of the page. At the bottom of most pages in the book, I added a little "iTip," which is just a cutesy name for extra bonus tips that make using your iPod easier or more fun. Most times, they relate to the technique shown on that page, but sometimes I had a really cool tip and nowhere specific to put it, so I just stuck it where I found a space. Hey, at least ya know.

(7) That all important "seventh thing." Okay, there's not really a seventh thing, but saying "Six things you'll need to know" just sounded so "weenie" I couldn't bring myself to write it. Seriously though, I hope you enjoy the book, and really dig into some of the very cool things you can do with your iPod, iTunes, and the iTunes Store. There are a lot more powerful and useful features there than you'd think—and that's a really good thing. So tear into it and have fun!

Chapter One

Start Me Up

Learning That Essential Stuff

 Since this is the first chapter of the book, it's only fair to let you know that the chapter titles in all my books are taken from movie, song, or TV show titles and, as I mentioned in the book's introduction, the chapter intros have little (or nothing) to do with the chapters that follow, but are designed to give you a mental break from the rest of the book. Since this is only the first chapter, you're probably wondering why you already need a break. I've asked myself that same question and, so far, I haven't come up with a reasonable answer. Anyway, this chapter is named for the Rolling Stones' song, which is a great song title for a chapter on where to start with your iPod. Sadly, I'm not the first to use this song—Microsoft used it for the launch of Windows 3 (shortly after the Spanish/American war), because it was the first version to have the Start menu, and the tie-in was too perfect to resist. In fact, they used the actual Stones' song itself in their TV commercials, which cost them a bundle. I hear it required not only a cash payment, but they had to sign the Treaty of Paris, which included ceding control of Cuba, the Philippines, Puerto Rico, and Guam to the Stones' record company for an undisclosed period of time, however, a report in Britain's *Yorkshire Pudding Post*, from an unnamed source, claimed the treaty didn't expire until the U.S. introduced the Monroe Doctrine, which opened a free trade route to Newark Liberty International Airport. See, I bet you didn't expect a highly accurate American history lesson to sneak into this now, did you?

Charging Your Battery (Using the USB Cable)

When you get an iPod, the first thing you need to do is charge the battery. Luckily, each iPod includes a white USB 2 cable that lets you charge it by plugging it into your computer. Here's how: Take the cable and insert the thin flat side into the slot at the bottom of your iPod. Then connect the other end of the cable to the USB port on your computer. That's it—your iPod is charging and you'll either see a big battery charging indicator icon or the Connected…Eject Before Disconnecting screen in its LCD display. If you need to disconnect, first eject your iPod by clicking on the little Eject icon that appears to the right of its name in the Devices list in iTunes. Then you can safely unplug it without damaging any music or video files.

---

iTip: Turning Your iPod On and Off

As silly as this may seem (how to turn it on and off), I can't tell you how many people get tripped up by this because there isn't an On/Off button. So, how do you turn it on? Press any button on the front of your iPod, and it will spring to life (so, in essence, every button is the On button). But it's not that way for turning the iPod off. To turn it off, press-and-hold the Play/Pause button for a couple of seconds and it will go to sleep.

Where iTunes Fits In

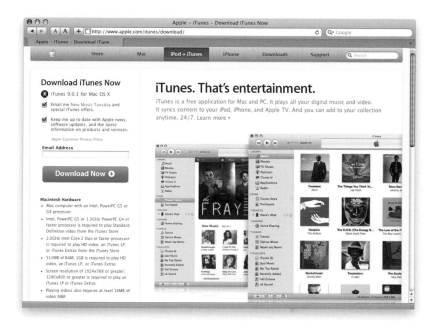

iTunes is the free software from Apple (for Windows PCs and Macintosh computers) that lets you manage (and even buy) the music, movies, and other content that winds up on your iPod. iTunes has a lot of really dedicated (okay, fanatical) fans because it's some of the coolest, most fun software ever made, and although it's easy to use, it's surprisingly powerful (there's a ton of stuff hidden under the surface), so a decent chunk of this book is dedicated to teaching you the ins and outs of iTunes, because it's where you'll spend a lot of your time. It's also the home of the iTunes Store, the world's largest and most popular online music store. This is basically how the process works: you import music and video files into iTunes (or download them from the iTunes Store), and then when you connect your iPod to your computer, iTunes launches and whatever music and videos you have in iTunes gets copied automatically over to your iPod. It sounds pretty simple, and it is, so let's get started. You can download the latest version of iTunes at **www.apple.com/itunes/download**.

Importing Songs from a CD

Launch Apple's iTunes software, then put a music CD into your computer's CD-ROM drive. The songs on your music CD will appear listed in the iTunes main window (if you're connected to the Internet, iTunes will automatically add the song titles for you. If it's not a commercial CD—maybe this is a mix CD you created, or a CD of a friend's band—your songs will appear with the generic names "Track 1," "Track 2," and so on). A dialog will appear asking, "Would you like to import the CD [name of CD] into your iTunes library?" Click the Yes button, and it copies all the songs on your CD onto your computer, and into iTunes. That's all there is to it. If there's a particular song on the CD you don't want imported, just turn off the checkbox that appears before its name. By the way, if you only want one song imported, click the No button, then press-and-hold the Command (PC: Ctrl) key, and click once on the checkbox beside the song you want. This unchecks all the songs. Now, click again on the checkbox beside the song you want to import, and click the **Import CD button** at the bottom right of iTunes.

---

iTip: Click the Import CD Button

If, for some reason, you don't get the little dialog asking if you want to import the songs from your CD into your iTunes Library, or you accidentally clicked the No button, you can always click the Import CD button in the bottom-right corner of iTunes.

Importing Songs Already on Your Computer

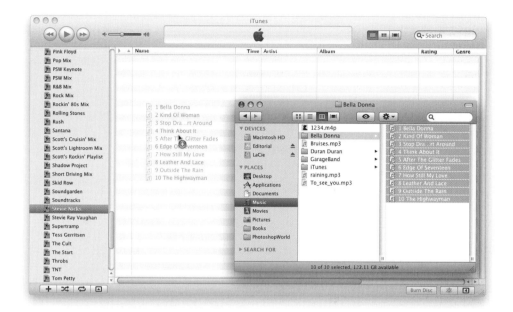

If you already have songs on your computer, getting them imported into iTunes is a breeze. You can literally drag-and-drop the songs from your computer right into the main iTunes window, and they'll be imported automatically. Or, you can go under the iTunes File menu and choose **Add to Library (PC: Add File or Folder to Library)**, which brings up a standard Open dialog. Find the songs (or videos) you want to import into iTunes, then click the Open button and iTunes brings them on in. If you're connected to the Internet while you're doing this, iTunes will even go and find the album art for the songs you've imported. Sweet!

---

iTip: When It's Okay to Just Unplug Your iPod

I always get questions about when it's okay to just unplug your iPod from your computer, and when you need to eject it first before unplugging. Rule #1: Always look at the display window at the top center of iTunes—it will tell you what to do. If it says "Do Not Disconnect," then don't disconnect yet. If it says "iPod sync is complete" with nothing written under it, you can just disconnect your iPod and off you go. Also, if you look at your iPod and you see your main menu, it's okay to disconnect. Rule #2: If you have your iPod set up to use as a flash drive (see Chapter 3), you will always need to eject it first. When it says "iPod sync is complete" in iTunes, under that it will say "Eject before disconnecting." (It will also say this on your iPod itself.)

Downloading Songs from the iTunes Store

The iTunes Store is the groundbreaking, history-making online store that started it all, and it's so well designed that it really makes shopping for music, movies, TV shows, podcasts, games, and videos an awful lot of fun. To get to the iTunes Store, launch the iTunes software on your computer, then click on the **iTunes Store link** on the left side of iTunes (shown circled in red above). (*Note:* This is an online store, so you have to have an Internet connection to access it.) There are so many cool features in the iTunes Store that I've dedicated an entire chapter to it (Chapter 9), but in short, here's how it works: you browse around the store looking for your favorite songs, movies, etc., and when you find something you want, you click the Buy button. You'll have to set up an account (it takes just a moment—and a credit card, of course), but then your download will begin and your song, movie, music video—whatever—will appear in your iTunes Library. The next time you connect your iPod, whatever you bought in the iTunes Store gets copied over onto your iPod. You do, however, have the option of listening to (or watching) your downloads either on your iPod or on your computer, right within iTunes itself.

Creating a Playlist

Once your music is imported into your iTunes Music Library, it's just kind of in one big bucket—it's not sorted or categorized. That's why there are playlists. You make playlists to bring some sort of organization to your music collection. For example, you might want to create a playlist of just your favorite rock songs, or just '70s disco, or just alternative, or classical, or a playlist of just a particular artist, or you might create a playlist of sad songs, or slow songs, or a mix for a party you're throwing, or just romantic songs, or just your kid's favorite songs (you get the idea). Creating playlists is simple: You start by clicking the **Create a Playlist button** at the bottom-left corner of iTunes (it's the plus sign). This adds an empty playlist to your list of playlists in the Source list on the left side of iTunes, and the name is already highlighted so you can type one in, then press the Return (PC: Enter) key on your keyboard. To add songs to this new playlist, under Library at the top left, click on Music, and then scroll through your collection. When you see a song you'd like in your playlist, just drag-and-drop that song title right onto your new playlist in the Source list, and it's added to it. Keep adding songs until you're done. Also, you can put your songs in any order you like within your playlist by simply dragging them into the position you want. Then, to play the songs in your playlist, click on it, double-click the first song, and the songs will play in order. If you double-click on the eighth song, it starts there instead and plays the rest of the songs in order until it reaches the end of the playlist (unless you have Repeat Playlist turned on. For more on playlists, see Chapter 8 and the PDF chapter I put online for you at **www.kelbytraining.com/books/ipod6**).

Getting Music onto Your iPod

When you've got your songs arranged in iTunes just the way you want them, you copy them over to your iPod using the white USB 2 cable that came with it. Just connect the cable to your iPod, then connect the other end to your computer, and it'll do the rest. The transfer is automatic—your computer will automatically launch iTunes and download your songs, playlists and all (unless you set it to Manually Manage Music and Videos [see Chapter 3]). Watch the display window at the top of iTunes, and when the transfer of songs is complete, you'll see the message, "iPod sync is complete." Click on the little Eject icon next to your iPod's name in the Devices list on the left to eject it from iTunes. Once it says "OK to Disconnect" in your iPod's screen, you can just unplug it and start listening (or watching).

---

iTip: Why Apple's iPod Dock Rocks

Perhaps the most convenient way to sync and charge your iPod is to get the Apple Universal Dock—you just sit your iPod in the Dock, and it syncs your iPod and charges it. There are four advantages to the Dock: (1) it's easier—because you don't have to connect the USB cable to the bottom of your iPod each time; (2) it puts your iPod upright, so you can see the screen, rather than just having it lying flat; (3) it comes with an Apple remote, so you can wirelessly control your iPod while it's in the Dock; and (4) the Dock has a line out port, so you can connect your iPod to your stereo speakers/receiver.

Getting Your New Songs onto Your iPod

If you've added new songs to iTunes (maybe you bought some songs from the iTunes Store or imported songs from a CD) or changed your playlists, you're going to want to get these new songs or playlists onto your iPod. To do that, connect your iPod to your computer (using the Dock or the supplied USB 2 cable), and iTunes will launch and automatically update your iPod with the new songs. If your iPod was already connected to your computer when you bought a new song (or imported songs from a CD), then just click the **Sync button** (shown circled above) and it'll update your iPod with the new songs.

---

iTip: My Favorite External Speakers

Although iPods were born to be used with headphones, today there are a lot of speaker systems custom-designed for iPods. In my opinion, the three hottest external speaker systems are the Bose SoundDock Series, $300–$600; the JBL On Stage, around $110; and the Sony ICF-C1iPMK2 Dock with Clock, around $100 (you can buy the first two at the Apple Store online). All three have a built-in cradle (it's like a Dock) that your iPod sits in while playing, and all automatically charge your iPod at the same time.

Using Your iPod nano or iPod classic

The iPod nano and the iPod classic are both controlled using the round Click Wheel on the front of the iPod. There are five buttons on the wheel: A Menu button at the top, a Play/Pause button at the bottom, a Rewind button on the left side, a Fast-Forward button on the right side, and a Center button that makes selections. You move through the iPod's menus by sliding your finger lightly around this wheel (like you're tracing a circle) in either a clockwise or counterclockwise motion. When you find something you want, you press the Center button.

---

iTip: Pausing a Song

If you're playing a song and you want to pause it, just press the Play/Pause button. Want to resume playing? Press the same button again. This button both plays and pauses, and that's why its icon has both the play and pause symbols.

Playing Songs, Volume, and Stuff Like That

To get to your music playlists, press-and-hold the Menu button to get to the main menu, choose Music, then choose **Playlists**, and you'll see a list of all the playlists you created on your computer in iTunes (and synced to your iPod). If you click on a playlist, it shows you the songs in it, and to hear any one of them, just click on it. Your song will begin playing, and when it's done, the next song in that playlist will play, and the next, and so on. To pause the song, press the **Play/Pause button** at the bottom of the Click Wheel. To restart the song, press the same button, again. To skip to the next song, press the **Fast-Forward button** once (I know I probably don't have to tell you this, but to hear the same song again, press the **Rewind button**, or press it twice to hear the previous song). A progress bar appears on-screen so you can see where you are in the song (closer to the end, closer to the beginning, in the middle, etc.). When you remove your finger from the Click Wheel, the song starts playing from that point. To change the volume, just glide your finger around the Click Wheel (to the right to raise it; to the left to lower it). The moment you start sliding either way, a volume bar appears, and this bar grows longer/shorter as you increase/decrease the volume.

---

iTip: Jumping Ahead or Back in Your Song (Scrubbing)

You can jump ahead or back in a song while it's playing (called "scrubbing") by pressing the Center button once, then slide your finger around the Click Wheel clockwise to scrub farther into the song (or counterclockwise to scrub back).

Playing Video on Your iPod

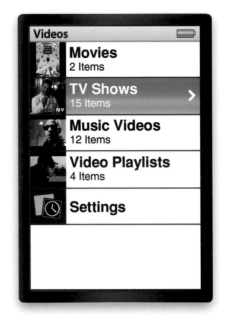

You can play TV shows, movies, video podcasts, and music videos that you download from the iTunes Store on your iPod nano or iPod classic. When you sync your iPod with iTunes on your computer, any videos you've purchased will be downloaded onto your iPod. You'll find these by going to the main menu and then clicking on **Videos**. (*Note:* Podcasts have their own menu.) In the Videos menu (shown above), scroll down to the type of video you want and click the Center button. For example, if you click on TV Shows, any TV shows you've downloaded will be listed here. To play a particular show, scroll down to it, then press the Center button to see a list of episodes. When you find the episode you're looking for, press the Play button (or just press the Center button again). While the video is playing, if you click the Center button once, it shows the time remaining and a volume bar; two clicks brings up a scrubber bar (for quickly scrolling forward or backward in the video); and three clicks brings up the Brightness control.

---

iTip: Create Video Playlists

Just like playlists for music, you can create playlists for videos, as well, with collections of your favorite TV shows, movies, or music videos. For example, you could create a video playlist of Michael Jackson videos, or videos of dance music, or classic rock videos, or... well, you get the idea.

Done Listening? Put It to Sleep

When you're done listening to your iPod for a while, you can put it to sleep two ways: (1) pause your music by pressing the **Pause button**, and after a minute or two of being paused, your iPod will go to sleep to save battery life; or (2) press-and-hold the Pause button for a few seconds, and it will go to sleep right away (your screen will turn black). Your iPod remembers where you were in a song when it went to sleep, so when you wake it later, it picks right back up where you left off. (Unless you leave your iPod asleep for 36 hours or more, in which case it falls into a deep sleep. If that happens, it starts up again from scratch—with the Apple splash screen and all—which takes longer than its normal wake-up, because it has to go through a little startup routine.)

---

iTip: A Good Way to Keep from Draining Your Battery

*After you put your iPod to sleep, before you just go tossing it into your pocket, purse, backpack, computer bag, etc., I recommend sliding the **Hold switch** (found on the top of the iPod) to the "on" position (so the orange part is visible). This locks the buttons on the Click Wheel, so if something accidentally bumps into it, it doesn't turn your iPod on, needlessly draining the battery.*

Turning On the Backlight

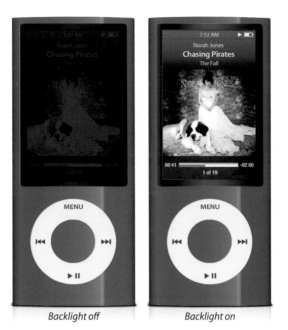

Backlight off   Backlight on

What do you do if you're in a dark, smoky London club on Playlist Night, but it's too dark in there to see your playlists (after all, it's not just dark—it's dark and smoky)? Here's what to do: just press anywhere on the Click Wheel and your iPod's Backlight will come on, illuminating your screen like a beacon in the night (please consider that last part marketing copy).

---

iTip: Stretch Your iPod Battery Life By Turning Down the Backlight

*The backlight is a major battery drainer, so if you limit how long it stays lit, you can really stretch your battery life big time. From the iPod nano's main menu, choose Settings, then click on General, then click on **Backlight**. On the iPod classic, when you're in the Settings menu, just click on Backlight. This brings up a screen with choices for how long your backlight will stay on—from two seconds (probably too short to be practical) to Always On (ideal for people who don't roam more than a few feet from their battery charger). Just find the setting that seems right for you and click on it.*

Controlling Your Screen's Brightness

The ability to change the brightness of your screen serves a major purpose—extending your battery life. That glorious full-color screen draws a lot of battery power, and if you don't need the screen at its full brightness (for example, you're on a flight at night and the cabin lights are dimmed), you can lower the brightness by quite a bit and extend your battery life. To control the brightness, on the iPod nano, under Settings, go under the General menu, then click on **Brightness**. On the iPod classic, go to the main menu, then go under Settings, and choose Brightness. There you'll find the Brightness slider. The default brightness is around 50%, so it ships from the factory at about half of its maximum brightness. You adjust the brightness level the same way you do volume—you scroll the Click Wheel to the right to make it brighter or to the left to make it less bright (and save even more battery life).

How's Your Battery Life?

Is it time to charge your battery? Just take a quick peek in the upper right-hand corner of the iPod's screen and you'll see a little battery indicator. If it's solid, you're in good shape. If it's half-full, then you're an optimist. (Get it? Half-full? Ah, forget it.) Actually it means it's got half of a full charge. If the battery indicator is clear, it means it's time to recharge your iPod battery by plugging it into your computer, or putting your iPod in the Apple Dock (provided you have one, of course).

Replacing Your iPod's Battery

Eventually your iPod's battery will reach the point of no return (it won't hold a charge any longer), and you'll have to get the battery replaced. Well, I have good news and bad news. The good news: even with lots of use, your iPod's battery will last for quite a while. The bad news: this isn't one of those "drive-down-to-Walmart-and-buy-a-new-battery-for-$4.99" situations. iPod batteries aren't cheap (as of the printing of this book, depending on the model, Apple charges $49–$79, plus shipping, for a new iPod replacement battery), and they should be replaced by a qualified technician (like a tech at the Apple Store in the mall). If you can't spring for the battery from Apple and the technician's fee for replacing it, you've got a few other options: There's also iResQ.com, where they'll give you a new iPod battery, do the install, and ship your iPod back to you within 24 hours (the shipping's included). Considering the cost, this is why it's a good idea to get AppleCare for your new iPod for around $59 ($39 for the nano or shuffle), which would cover not only mechanical failures, but also a battery replacement if you needed one.

Chapter Two

Nano-Nucleonic Cyborg Summoning

Using Your iPod nano or classic

▶▶ This may well be the worst chapter name ever, but you have to realize, there aren't a lot of songs with the word "nano" in the title. There are plenty of song titles with the word "classic" in them, but way more people use iPod nanos these days (the built-in video camera and larger screen are hard to resist), so I went the nano route. Now, the title above is actually an album title (which technically violates a long-standing chapter intro song title tradition of mine, but I checked with the judges, and they agreed to let this one slide, because in Article 6, Section 11, of my indiscernible publishing contract, it clearly states that "said title may be interpreted except to the extent that a material and prejudicial change of position prior to acquiring knowledge or reason to know of misappropriation renders a reasonable song title usage inequitable." So, I think that grants me a pretty wide berth to use an album title). Anyway, the album is from the tech-metal band Behold…The Arctopus (I didn't add "Behold…" for dramatic flair—that's actually part of their name). From the iTunes reviews, people seem to like them, and I see why. Their album includes not only the song "Alcoholocaust," but a separate live version, as well, and you know what they say, "You haven't heard 'Alcoholocaust' until you've heard it live." Personally, I think the guitar work on their track "Estrogen/Pathogen Exchange Program" is unspeakably brilliant and connects with the listener in a way that "Sensory Amusia" never could. By the way, I have no idea what any of that means.

Customizing the Main Menu

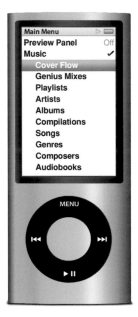

The iPod has a main menu that is kind of the starting place for making your way around the different areas of your iPod. You'll wind up using this main menu a lot, and that's why you'll want to customize it so the features you use most are right there at the top level (reducing your need to dig down through different menus). Here's how to customize yours: Start at the main menu and, using the Click Wheel, scroll down to Settings and press the Center button. Now, on the iPod nano, scroll to General, press the Center button again, then scroll to **Main Menu** and press the Center button once more to see a list of menu items. You can choose which ones you want to appear in your main menu by toggling them on or off using the Center button (items with a checkmark beside them will appear in the main menu). On an iPod classic, you'll find Main Menu under Settings.

---

iTip: Getting to the Main Menu

*With the iPod, everything pretty much starts at the main menu, and since you'll find yourself going back there fairly often, you might as well learn how to get there at any time—just press-and-hold the **Menu button** and you'll be back at the main menu. Think of it like a "back" button.*

Searching for Songs Made Easy

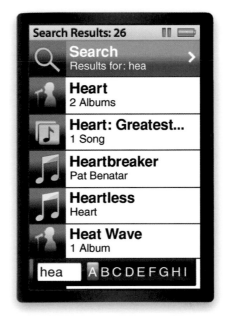

The iPod has a Search feature to help find the song (or artist or album) you're looking for fast. Press-and-hold the Menu button to jump to the main menu, click on Music, then scroll down and click on **Search**. When the Search menu appears, you'll see the alphabet near the bottom of the window. Scroll to the first letter of the song, or album name, or artist's name, then click the Center button, and it instantly starts searching and gives you results live as you enter each subsequent letter. For example, if you're looking for Heart, as soon as you select H, it instantly (and I mean instantly) lists every song, or album, or artist on your iPod that begins with "H." When you move over to E and press the Center button, now it's every song, or album, or artist that begins with "He." By the time you press A, you've narrowed your search down pretty well (on my iPod, it lists Heart and then "Heartbreaker" by Pat Benatar). If you choose a wrong letter, you can use the Rewind button to delete it, and if you need to put a space between words, press the Fast-Forward button. When you're done searching, press the Menu button, and the search bar goes away, but your search results remain in the window. Now you can just click on the song, or album, or artist you want.

Visual Searching with Cover Flow

If you're a visual person, rather than scrolling through a list to find the song you want, try using Cover Flow. It displays the album cover art of the songs on your iPod (as shown above) and it's designed to kind of digitally recreate the experience of looking through a stack of albums at the record store. If you have an iPod nano, you can just turn it on its side, and it will switch to Cover Flow view. If you have an iPod classic, then start at the main menu, select Music, and click on **Cover Flow**. Once you're in Cover Flow view, slide your finger around the Click Wheel to scroll through your entire Music Library and just stop when you see the album you want. Technically, it's probably not faster than searching by name, but it's definitely way more fun.

---

iTip: Using Your iPod as a Stopwatch

*Press-and-hold the Menu button to jump to the main menu, scroll down and click on Extras, then scroll down to **Stopwatch** and click on it. To start it, just press the Center button; to stop it, press the Play/Pause button. On an iPod nano, press the Menu button for options (on an iPod classic, you'll already see them on the screen) for where you can choose to restart the timer, clear the log of laps (each time you start and stop the stopwatch, the iPod automatically logs it—to see the full list in detail, with stats, click on Current Log), or create an entirely new timer.*

Shuffling Your Song Order

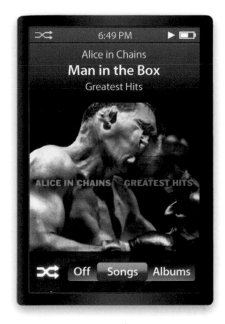

To turn on the iPod's Shuffle feature, which plays your songs in a totally random order (you can either shuffle all the songs in your Music Library, or just songs in your current playlist), press-and-hold the Menu button to jump to the main menu, then scroll down and click on **Shuffle Songs** to turn this feature on. If you're in a playlist, playing a song, and you decide you want to shuffle that playlist, press the Center button four times in a row and a shuffle control bar will appear at the bottom of the song window (as seen above). You can use the Click Wheel to choose Songs (which shuffles by song title), Albums (to shuffle by album), or Off.

Shake Your nano to Turn on Shuffle

Apple includes a cool feature in the iPod nano that allows you to shuffle your songs by simply shaking it. This feature utilizes a built-in accelerometer. Start a song playing from your Music Library or a playlist and, once you get to a point that you want to hear a new song, literally shake your iPod nano side to side a couple of times and it should start playing a new song (since it shuffles, your iPod will randomly pick a new song from your Music Library or playlist). Now, if you're worried that this feature could get in your way (for example, while jogging), you can turn it off in the Settings. From the main menu, scroll down to Settings and press the Center button, then click on Playback. Scroll down to **Shake** and press the Center button once to turn this "shake-to-shuffle" off. *Note:* This also works on the iPod touch. To turn it off, from the Home screen, tap on Settings, then tap on Music, and tap the On/Off button next to Shake to Shuffle.

Repeating the Current Song or Playlist

If you're really hung up on a song, press-and-hold the Menu button to jump to the main menu, scroll down, click on Settings, then scroll to **Repeat**. Press the Center button to choose All and repeat the current playlist; press it again, to choose One and repeat only the current song; press it one more time to turn it back off (on an iPod classic, you'll get the One option first, then the All option).

---

iTip: Which File Formats Work with Your iPod

Music you buy from the iTunes Store comes in AAC format, which compresses the file size (so you can fit more songs on your iPod), while maintaining nearly CD quality. The songs you download from the Web are probably in MP3, M4A, or M4B, but the iPod supports those, too! If you download other formats (like WMA files), when you import them, iTunes will convert them automatically into whichever format you have chosen in your Import Settings dialog (go into iTunes' Preferences, click on General up top, and click on the Import Settings button), so they will play on your iPod.

Rating Your Favorites

Even though you probably have a lot of songs on your iPod, they're not all "your favorite song." Obviously, you like some better than others, and choosing which ones you like best (rating them from one to five stars) can be very helpful in making sure you hear your favorites more often. That's because once you've rated your songs, you can sort them so that your favorites (five stars) play first, then your next favorites (four stars), and so on. (Better yet, you can create a smart playlist where iTunes automatically compiles just your four- and five-star songs—more on that in Chapter 8!) You can rate your songs in iTunes, or right from your iPod while they're playing. Just press the Center button three times and five little dots will appear at the bottom of the screen. Scroll the Click Wheel clockwise to add stars, and counterclockwise to take them away.

---

iTip: Updating Your Ratings

If you're rating your songs, it doesn't matter where you rate them—whether it's within iTunes or right on your iPod—because the next time you sync your iPod and iTunes, any new ratings (no matter where they came from) are synced between them. Your ratings will then be updated in both places automatically, so they're always up to date. Cool, ain't it?

Creating a Playlist Right on Your iPod (On-The-Go)

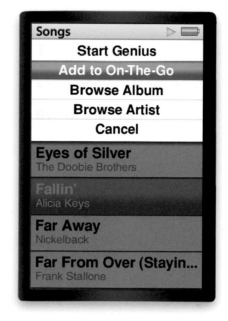

We normally create playlists in iTunes, but you can create custom "On-The-Go" playlists right on your iPod. To add a song to it, scroll to a song and press-and-hold the Center button. From the menu, choose **Add to On-The-Go**. When you're done, you'll find this song in the On-The-Go playlist at the bottom of the Playlists menu. To remove a song from it, you do the same thing you did to add it—scroll to the song and press-and-hold the Center button, but this time, choose **Remove from On-The-Go**. To save it as a regular playlist, choose **Save Playlist** (from the top of the On-The-Go menu), which clears your On-The-Go Playlist, so you can create a new one. To clear your On-The-Go playlist and start over, choose **Clear Playlist** (again, from the top of the On-The-Go menu). When you sync your iPod with your computer, your new On-The-Go playlist will appear in iTunes, and you can add songs, delete songs, and reorder them just like you would any other playlist.

---

iTip: Adding an Album to Your On-The-Go Playlist

You can add more than one song at a time to your On-The-Go playlist. In fact, you can add an entire album, or all the songs from a particular artist. Just find the album or artist on your iPod, press-and-hold the Center button, choose Add to On-The-Go from the menu, and all those songs are added.

Make a Genius Playlist on Your iPod

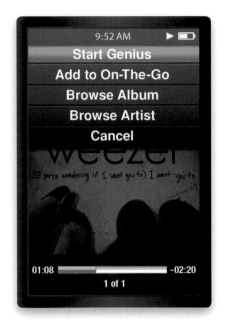

A Genius playlist is one that your iPod creates for you based on a song you choose (it figures out which other songs would go well with the song you've chosen). You select a song or start one playing first and then press-and-hold the Center button. When the menu appears, choose **Start Genius**, which will create a Genius playlist based on your chosen song. You'll find the Genius playlist right along with your other playlists. By the way, there is one thing you have to do first for this to work: you have to have the Genius feature turned on in iTunes by clicking on the Genius button at the bottom right (see Chapter 8 for more on turning on the Genius feature). If you want to save this as a regular playlist, just choose **Save Playlist** from the Genius screen.

---

iTip: Turning Off the Click Sound

*While you're scrolling around through the menus, your iPod makes an audible "click" sound, so you know "things are happening." If you want that click turned off, on an iPod nano, start at the main menu, then scroll down to Settings, choose General, and then click on **Clicker** to turn the scrolling sound off. Press the Center button again to turn it back on. On the iPod classic, after you get to Settings, you'll find Clicker.*

Enhancing Your Sound Quality (EQ)

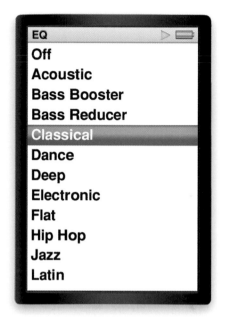

You're about to uncover a feature of your iPod that can make your music sound so much better, you'll never turn it off again (and sadly, it's off by default). Your iPod has a built-in sound equalizer that can change the audio output of your iPod so it sounds best for the type of music you listen to—and best of all, all you have to do is choose from a list of built-in presets. Here's how it works: On an iPod nano, press-and-hold the Menu button to jump to the main menu, scroll down to Settings, and press the Center button, then choose Playback, then choose **EQ**. On the iPod classic, after you get to Settings, you'll find EQ. When you click on EQ, you'll see a list of preset EQs for various musical genres (e.g., R&B, Hip Hop, Jazz, Spoken Word, Acoustic, Classical, etc., plus special EQ settings that boost or reduce the bass or treble, or boost the vocals). Just scroll down to the type of music you listen to, click the Center button, then go back and listen to your music again. You'll be absolutely amazed at how much richer, fuller, and just flat-out better it will sound.

---

iTip: Add a Clock to Your Song Window

*You can have your iPod display the current time while you're playing a song. To do that, start at the main menu and click on Settings. Scroll down and click on Date & Time, and when the Date & Time menu of options appears, click on **Time in Title** to turn this feature on. Now the current time will appear up in the left-hand side of your Title Bar when playing a song (this is on by default on the iPod classic).*

Saving Your Ears from Volume Abuse

Since the recorded volume of songs can vary greatly from song to song, luckily, there's an iPod feature called Sound Check that automatically balances the volume between songs, so you don't suddenly get your ears blasted right off your head. This ear-saving feature, however, is turned off by default—you have to go turn it on. Here's how: On an iPod nano, press-and-hold the Menu button to jump to the main menu, scroll down and click on Settings, choose Playback, then scroll down to **Sound Check**. On the iPod classic, after you get to Settings, you'll find Sound Check. Click the Center button once to turn it on (the Off to the right of Sound Check will change to On).

Finding Out How Much Space Is Left for More Songs and Videos

If you're wondering how many more songs or videos you can fit on your iPod, here's a quick way to find out: From the main menu, scroll down and click on Settings. Then, on the Settings menu, click on **About** to see a horizontal bar graph of your iPod's available memory. If you want to see exactly how many songs and videos are on your iPod, then click the Center button again.

---

iTip: Using iTunes to Check Free Space

Another way to know how much room is left on your iPod for adding more songs and videos is to check in iTunes. When your iPod is connected to your computer, just click on its icon in the Source list on the left side of the window. Then look down along the bottom center of the main window and you'll see a readout that shows how much space is used, and how much space is still free for adding more songs or videos.

Deleting a Song from Your iPod

If a song you really hate winds up sneaking its way onto your iPod (this sometimes happens to a song you liked at one time, but after a few dozen plays, it really starts to get on your nerves), you can delete it from your iPod. Well, you actually have to delete it in iTunes and the easiest way is to delete the song from your iTunes playlist—just click on the song, press Delete (PC: Backspace), then click **Remove**. Plug in your iPod into your computer, and when the iPod syncs, the offending song is gone!

---

iTip: Renaming Your iPod

If you want to give your iPod a new name, first connect your iPod to your computer. Let's say, for example, that you want to change the name of your iPod to "Scott Kelby's iPod." (Hey, don't laugh. That's what I named mine and I kinda like it.) Click directly on its name under Devices (in the Source list) and its name field will highlight, ready for you to type in a new name (it's spelled "S-c-o-t-t"). Press the Return (PC: Enter) key on your keyboard when you're done.

Listening to Audiobooks on Your iPod

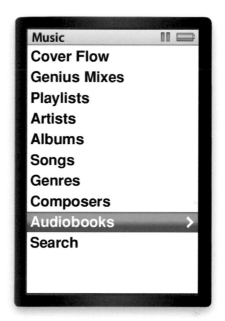

The next time you're taking a trip, you might want to consider taking along a few audio-books. Not only is the iPod designed to play audiobooks, but the iTunes Store also sells them. (The iPod supports audiobooks downloaded from Audible.com, as well.) To buy an audiobook, go to the iTunes Store, then click the **Audiobooks link** at the top of the main window. If you find a title you like and download it, when you sync your iPod, you'll find your audiobook by starting at the main menu, choosing Music, and pressing the Center but-ton. Then scroll all the way down to the bottom, where you'll find **Audiobooks**. Also, in case you were wondering, when you stop listening to an audiobook, your iPod notes the spot where you stopped, so when you go back to it at a later date, it picks up right where you left off (kind of like a digital bookmark). Better yet, this feature also works in iTunes—even when you sync it with your iPod, they update each other, keeping track of where you left off.

---

iTip: Changing Narration Speed

*With audiobooks, you'll learn that sometimes the narrator's pace is just right, sometimes it's too slow, and sometimes it's too fast. Luckily, you can change that. On an iPod nano, from the main menu, scroll down to Settings and press the Center button. Then scroll down to Playback, press the Center button again, and then scroll to **Audiobooks**. (On an iPod classic, from the main menu, you'll just scroll to Settings and then to Audiobooks.) Normal, thankfully, is the default speed of audiobooks, but to speed things up, click on the Center button to choose Faster, or to slow them down, choose Slower.*

Setting an Alarm

Want to make sure you get to traffic court on time? Use your iPod's alarm function. Start at the main menu, scroll down to Extras, click on Alarms, then click on **Create Alarm**, and now your iPod's alarm will sound—you just don't know when. Luckily, there's a list of alarm options where you can choose the date and time you want this alarm to go off, whether you want it to repeat, and you even get to choose the alert sound your iPod will wake you with (either an audible beep or a playlist of songs [if you choose the playlist option, you'll need to connect your iPod classic to an external set of speakers, so you can actually hear your wake-up playlist]). You can also assign a label to your alarm to help you see at a glance which alarm you've set is for what, and you can delete an existing alarm here, as well. Okay, your alarm is set. At the time you specified, your iPod will "alarm" you.

---

iTip: Tracking Multiple Time Zones

*If you want to keep track of multiple time zones for different parts of the world (you international jet-setter, you), then click on **Clocks** (found under the Extras menu), and now you can view different clocks monitoring different time zones. Click the Center button then choose Add to add a new city, Edit to change the selected city to something else, or Delete to remove it.*

Your iPod Has Three Built-In Games

Your iPod comes with a few cute little games already installed. To get to them, start at the main menu, scroll down and choose Extras, then scroll down to **Games** and press the Center button. The built-in games are Klondike (a version of Solitaire), Vortex, and Maze on a nano or iQuiz on a classic. Press the Center button to choose a game and watch the hours just fly by. Of course, you can buy much better games (including classic arcade games like Pac-Man), from your computer using iTunes. Start by clicking on the iTunes Store link (on the left side of iTunes), then move your cursor up over the App Store button and click the down-facing arrow beside it, and from the menu, choose **iPod Click Wheel Games**. The iPod Click Wheel Games window will appear (don't get too excited—there aren't a whole bunch), and to learn more about a game, click on it. To buy it, click the Buy Game button. (*Note:* You can't play these games in iTunes—they only play on your iPod.) After you buy an iPod game from the iTunes Store, connect your iPod to your computer to sync your new game by clicking on your iPod in the Source list, then clicking on the Games tab, where you'll see the games you own. Turn on the Sync Games checkbox and click the Apply button. Once a game is on your iPod, you can play it by looking under Games (you use the Click Wheel as your game controller).

Creating Voice Memos on Your iPod nano

To record a voice memo, start at the main menu, then go to Extras, and click on **Voice Memos**. On the Click Wheel, press the Play/Pause button and begin talking into the microphone on the back of your iPod nano—the same one it uses when you shoot video—and it will record whatever you say. It helps to make sure your fingers aren't over the mic itself—it's right above the camera. A red bar appears across the top of the screen that says "Recording." To pause your recording, press the Play/Pause button again, and a menu appears where you can choose to Resume recording, Delete your recording, or Stop and Save (you can record up to two hours in one single recording). When you stop your recording, it brings up the Voice Memos screen, where you can choose to record a new memo, or see the ones you've recorded. When you choose Voice Memos, it displays a list of your voice recordings (along with the time and date each was recorded, and how long each memo lasts). To hear a voice memo, choose it, and then choose Play. To delete a memo, choose Delete. You can also assign names to your saved memos (like interview, lecture, idea, etc.) by choosing Label. One nice feature is that when you sync your iPod nano to your computer, it will copy your voice memos over into iTunes for you into a Voice Memos playlist.

Listening to Your iPod nano's FM Radio

Before you can listen to your iPod nano's radio, you'll need to plug in the headphones that came with it, because inside the cable is the antennae it needs to receive the FM signal. Then, go to the main menu and click on **Radio**, then click the Play/Pause button on the Click Wheel. Now you can rotate your finger around the Click Wheel to choose which station (on the radio dial) you want to listen to (of course, you're going to get the best reception on closer stations and those with a strong signal). If you press-and-hold the Fast-Forward or Rewind buttons on the Click Wheel, it'll scan stations with a decent signal. When it finds one, it plays it for a few a seconds, then moves on. To manually jump ahead or back to the next station on the dial, press the Fast-Forward or Rewind button once. If you find a station you like, press-and-hold the Center button and a menu appears where you can choose to add it as a Favorite (kind of like when you save stations on your car radio). Now when you press Fast-Forward or Rewind, it jumps straight to stations you've marked as Favorites (the name of the station will have a Favorites star to the top right of it).

---

iTip: Getting Back to the Radio Dial

When you're working with the radio, if you get lost, to quickly get back to the Radio dial, just keep pressing the Center button until the dial appears.

Pausing Live FM Radio on Your iPod nano

If you're listening to a station and have to stop to do something else, you can press the Play/Pause button (on the Click Wheel) to pause the live FM station you were listening to (it will stay paused for up to 15 minutes), and then pick up where you left off by pressing the Play/Pause button again (it actually records the station—kind of like what a DVR does for your TV). When you pause a station, a pop-up appears letting you know exactly what time it was paused. When you press Play/Pause again, it begins right where you paused it. You can jump ahead—one minute at a time—by pressing the Center button until a progress bar appears (where you see that pop-up with the time you paused it), then pressing the Fast-Forward button. You can do this up to 15 times, until you catch up with the live broadcast. If you don't do anything, after 15 minutes it deletes your pause and picks up with the live broadcast.

---

iTip: Buying Songs You Hear on Your iPod nano's Radio

A number of radio stations now support a thing called "iTunes Tagging," and what that means is when you hear a song on the FM radio you think you'd like to buy, and it's available for tagging (you'll see the title and artist beneath the station's call sign with a little tag icon to the right), just press-and-hold the Center button and choose **Tag** *from the menu. When you sync your iPod nano to your computer, it creates a Tagged playlist of these songs (under Store in the Source list), with a direct link to them in the iTunes Store, where you can preview them or buy them on the spot.*

Exercising with Your iPod nano

The iPod nano comes with a built-in pedometer, so it makes a great walking (or running) partner, because it'll automatically count your steps (and, ya know, it plays your favorite music for you, too). If you have an iPod nano arm band, put your iPod nano inside it before you start your walk/run, or if don't have one, you can just stick it in your pocket. But before you do this, from the main menu, scroll to Extras, then click on Fitness, and choose Settings. This is where you enter your weight (if you lie, your iPod nano will probably start laughing hysterically), how many steps you want as your daily step goal, choose your screen orientation, and choose if you always want the Pedometer on, or just on when you turn it on (that way, it can track your steps all day, or just during workout time). Now press the Menu button, choose **Pedometer**, press the Center button and it starts an exercise session (well, it starts tracking your steps anyway). To stop your session, just press the Center button again. The pedometer keeps a running history of your progress, and you can see how you did each day by choosing History from the Fitness menu, then clicking on a calendar day.

---

iTip: Getting the Full Nike + iPod nano Workout

If you're really serious about working out, you'll probably want the Nike + iPod Sport Kit for your iPod nano. See Chapter 6 for how it works on the iPod touch. It works similarly here, but you'll need to attach the receiver to your iPod nano (it's built into the iPod touch).

Getting Your iPod nano to Talk to You

Once a song is playing, you can have your iPod nano tell you the title and artist of the current song by just pressing the Center button—you'll hear it speak the title and artist (using its built-in, kind-of computery sounding voice). If, for some reason, yours doesn't, then just connect your iPod nano to your computer, and click on it under Devices in the iTunes Source list. On the Summary tab in the main window, under Voice Feedback, turn on the checkbox for **Enable VoiceOver** (as shown here). Now click the Apply button (in the bottom-right corner of the window) to let your iPod nano know you turned it on.

Chapter Three

It's Tricky
Cool iPod Tips & Tricks

Using a Run-D.M.C. song as the name of a chapter on iPod tips and tricks gets me some props, some street cred, because no matter how young and cool some of my readers might be, they can't dis Run-D.M.C. They helped put rap on the map, and rappers of all ages still give them respect. (Notice how I used the terms "props," "street cred," and "dis" in the opening? I did that as a shout-out to my homies and peeps. See, there I go again, using that hip street talk all the kids are using these days.) Look, here's the deal: When you're a middle-aged white guy, all you remember are the slang terms used when you were growing up. Then you start listening to stations like Mix 100.7 and Oldies 104, and you never hear new street slang again. So, the old street slang still sounds "new" to you and when you're in a situation where you're desperate to sound cool again (as I clearly am here), you instantly revert to words you remember were once cool. Like "props" and "dis." You might even throw in an occasional "chillin'," or if you're really old, you might actually call someone a "jive turkey" (believe it or not, there was a time when people under the age of 18 would use that term [with a straight face], and other people would think they were cool). So now I just sit around listening to old Salt-N-Pepa songs and repeating every cliché ever uttered on early editions of *Yo! MTV Raps*. Well, gotta go—my posse's hookin' up with another suck'a crew. (Forgive me.)

Using Your iPod as a Removable Hard Disk

The title here is kind of misleading, because your iPod actually is a hard disk, so it's not like you're fooling it into believing it's a hard disk—it already knows it is. However, for it to act like a regular hard disk (where you can store data, text files, Photoshop files, videos, etc.), you have to tell it that it's okay to do this. Start by connecting your iPod to your computer, and the Preferences Summary tab will automatically appear. In the Options section, turn on the checkbox for **Enable Disk Use**. (*Note:* You only need to turn this option on when you've chosen to automatically update your iPod. Otherwise, if you've chosen to update your iPod manually, the Enable Disk Use feature is on by default. See the next page for more on this.) Your iPod will now appear on your desktop, and you can add files by dragging-and-dropping them onto the iPod icon, just like any other removable hard disk. This is great for moving non-music files between machines. There's one thing to remember, though: when it's in this "disk" mode, you have to eject your iPod manually by Right-clicking on the iPod icon (either on your desktop or in the iTunes Source list) and choosing Eject in the contextual menu that appears.

Stopping Your iPod from Syncing Every Time

Each time you connect your iPod to your computer, iTunes automatically syncs your music and videos so your iPod is always up-to-date with what's in iTunes. If you'd prefer to update your iPod manually instead (so it doesn't automatically sync each time you plug it in), do this: While your iPod is connected to your computer, click on its icon under Devices on the left side of iTunes, and in the Summary tab, turn on the checkbox for **Manually Manage Music and Videos**. Now you're in charge of syncing. To update your iPod manually, just drag a song or video from your iTunes Music or Movies Library (at the top of the Source list on the left) and drop it on your iPod or one of your iPod's playlists.

Troubleshooting: Your iPod Won't Turn On

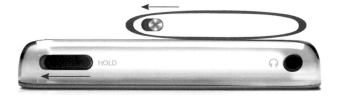

If your iPod won't turn on, most likely it's one of two things: (1) Check to see if the Hold switch (on top of the iPod) is turned on. If it is, all buttons are locked. Slide it over, so you don't see the orange indicator any longer (which unlocks all the buttons), then press any button to turn on your iPod. If that doesn't do the trick, then go to Plan B: (2) It's probably the battery. Try plugging your iPod into your computer using the USB 2 cable. If neither of these two solutions works, try resetting your iPod (using the instructions on the next page).

What to Do If Your iPod Locks Up

If your iPod locks up (meaning, it's on, but you can't get it to do anything—you're stuck on a screen and the buttons don't do anything, the Click Wheel doesn't click, etc.), you can reset it, which will usually do the trick (don't worry—resetting won't erase your songs, videos, or playlists). To reset your iPod, just slide the **Hold switch** (that button on top of your iPod) over to the lock position (so the bright orange color shows), and then slide it back again to unlock it. Now press-and-hold both the **Menu button** and the **Center button** until the Apple logo appears in the LCD window (this usually takes less than 10 seconds), then release both buttons.

Use Your iPod as a Contact Manager

You can store all your contacts on your iPod, as well. If you're on a Mac and you're using Apple's Address Book application (which comes with every Mac), just connect your iPod to your Mac (which launches iTunes). Click on your iPod in the Devices list on the left side, then on the Contacts tab in the main window, turn on the **Sync Address Book Contacts checkbox** (you can synchronize all of your contacts, or selected groups only). Now click Apply to sync your contacts with your iPod. If you're using a Windows PC, when you turn on the **Sync Contacts From checkbox** in iTunes, you'll have to choose which program to synchronize with (Windows Address Book, Outlook, etc.) from the adjacent pop-up menu, then click Apply to sync your contacts with your iPod. Now you'll find your contacts on your iPod by starting at the main menu, then going under Extras and choosing **Contacts**.

---

iTip: Importing Your Calendar

You can also import your calendar if you use either Apple's iCal or Microsoft Entourage on a Mac or Microsoft Outlook on a PC. Connect your iPod to your computer, click on it under Devices on the left side of iTunes, and turn on the **Sync Calendars checkbox** on the Contacts tab. To see your calendar info on your iPod, from the main menu, click on Extras, then click on Calendars, and click on **All Calendars**.

Safeguard Your iPod with Screen Lock

Screen Lock enables you to lock your iPod's screen using password protection, so if it were to fall into the hands of some scurrilous ne'er-do-well (a thief, or worse—your little brother), the screen would be locked, rendering it pretty much useless. To turn this feature on, start at the main menu, then go under the Extras menu, and select **Screen Lock**. First, you'll want to set your combination (numeric password): Selecting Lock brings up a screen where you use the Click Wheel to choose the numbers you want as your passcode (you press the Center button to confirm your first number, and it automatically highlights the next number field over, but you can also move from field to field using the Rewind and Fast-Forward buttons). Once you finish entering all four digits of your passcode, you'll be asked to confirm those numbers (yup—you have to enter all four digits again), and if you confirm all four numbers correctly, it takes you back to the Screen Lock menu, where you get to choose whether to lock your iPod or reset the passcode (which turns the locking off). If you choose Lock, it shows a large lock icon onscreen. To unlock your screen, press the Center button and enter your passcode.

---

iTip: If You Forget Your Passcode

If you forget your passcode, all is not lost. Just connect your iPod to your computer, and when it syncs, it automatically unlocks your iPod, because after all—it knows it's you. By the way, if someone enters the wrong passcode, they'll get an Incorrect Combination message, and the lock icon will reappear.

A Playlist Just on Your iPod but Not in iTunes

If there's a playlist that you want to appear just on your iPod (maybe it's a playlist you use when jogging, and you never play it in iTunes while sitting at your desk eating a Snickers), just connect your iPod to your computer, then turn on the manual update feature (covered earlier in this chapter). Now, click on your iPod in the Source list on the left side of iTunes and click on the right-facing triangle to its left to show a list of the playlists already on your iPod. Click on the **Create a Playlist button** in the bottom left-hand corner, and a new empty playlist will appear on your iPod within that list, with the name field already highlighted. So, type in a name, then press the Return (PC: Enter) key on your keyboard to lock it in. Now drag-and-drop songs directly into this "iPod Only!" playlist, knowing that this playlist will appear only on your iPod and won't be adding useless clutter to your regular list of playlists in iTunes (being the neat freak that you are).

Chapter Four

Video Killed the Radio Star

Video on Your iPod nano or classic

Okay, I admit the title for this chapter, a chapter on using video (TV shows, movies, and music videos) on your iPod, is just too obvious. But this song, lame as it was (is), has an important place in pop music history, for it was in fact this song that was the first video ever played on MTV. That's right, when MTV first aired, they aired the music video for the Buggles' "Video Killed the Radio Star." Now, if you've never heard this song, it's worth downloading from the iTunes Store and listening to (once) in iTunes. However, I don't recommend listening to it while driving (if you have your iPod connected to your car audio system), because it will subconsciously make you want to drive your car straight into the nearest stationary object. But, besides being a catchy-sounding name for this chapter, how does this song title relate to what's in this chapter? Well, it actually relates to a real-life story. I was producing a radio podcast (along with my cohorts, Dave Cross and Matt Kloskowski) called "Photoshop Radio" and each week we'd share Photoshop tips along with some of the lamest attempts at humor ever recorded digitally. However, when video podcasting came along, and Apple made iPods with video playback capabilities, we killed the radio show and started *Photoshop® User TV*. So, in effect, video killed our radio podcast. Now, I know what you want to ask, "Okay, that makes sense, but how does your real-life story relate to this chapter?" Actually, I was hoping you wouldn't ask that.

Buying and Renting Movies from the iTunes Store

Start by clicking on the iTunes Store link on the left side of iTunes, then click on the Movies link at the top of the Store homepage to take you to the main Movies page (if you already know which type of movie you're looking for, instead click to the right of Movies, and a pop-up menu of genres will appear so you can jump to the genre you want). As you scroll down the page, you'll see new videos, free videos, and a number of different categories highlighted (and a list of top sellers and rentals on the right). Click on any cover to see more about a movie—you can watch the trailer there, too (click the View Trailer button). If you want to buy the movie, click the **Buy Movie button** (the price is right on the button), and it will be downloaded onto your computer (and copied over onto your iPod the next time you sync it). If the movie can be rented, you'll also see a **Rent Movie button** with a lower price (it's a 30-day rental, but once you start watching it, you have 24 hours from that point to watch it as many times as you'd like—on your computer or on your iPod).

---

iTip: Downloading Music Videos from the iTunes Store

There are plenty of new (and classic) music videos for sale in the iTunes Store, and to find them, click to the right of the Music link up top, and then choose Music Videos from the pop-up menu. When you click on an individual video, you get much more info, and you can watch a 30-second preview of the video.

Downloading TV Shows
from the iTunes Store

TV shows are available from the iTunes Store, as well, and you get to them pretty much the same way you get to movies—click on the iTunes Store link on the left side of iTunes, then click on the TV Shows link at the top of the Store homepage (like with the Movies link, you can click to the right of it for a menu of TV show genres). There are loads of TV shows to buy here—you just click on the show you want, which takes you to an info page where you can watch a 30-second preview, or buy it and download it to your computer, and then to your iPod, if you want. There are also a ton of absolutely free episodes—just look for the Free TV Episodes button on the main TV Shows page. If you decide to buy a TV show, you can choose individual episodes or a Season Pass, so you get the entire season—once an episode airs, it will automatically be added to your Downloads queue, so you can download it when you're ready to watch it (just click the **Buy Season Pass button**). Some shows don't have a regular season, like E!'s *The Soup* or some specialized news shows, so those shows use a Multi-Pass instead, where you get a set number of shows for one price.

---

iTip: Playing a Video from Right Within iTunes Itself

iTunes has a built-in video player—just double-click on a movie, TV show, music video, or podcast you've downloaded, and it will start to play in your iTunes window with a set of controls appearing along the bottom of the screen (they disappear after a few seconds—to bring them back, just move your cursor over the video again).

A Faster Way to Find Videos in the Store

If you go to the iTunes Store, and you know the name of the TV show or movie you're looking for, you can save yourself a lot of wasted time digging through the various menus until you find the one you're after if you just use the Search Store field in the top-right corner of iTunes. For example, if you're trying to find the TV show *Flash Forward*, just go to the iTunes Store, and go right to the field and enter "Flash Forward." It will instantly bring up every song, podcast, album, app, TV show, and video with "Flash Forward" as a part of the title. Just glance in the TV Seasons or TV Episodes section, and you'll find it right there—just one click away. By the way, your iPod's built-in Search feature works differently. It only searches for songs on your iPod—not movies, TV shows, or music videos.

---

iTip: How to Tell It's a Music Video

If you buy a music video from the iTunes Store, when it downloads into iTunes, it appears in the Music Videos smart playlist, but it also appears in your Music Library along with your audio files. So, how you do know which items in your Music Library are songs and which are music videos? If it's a music video, iTunes puts a little TV screen icon to the right of the item's name, so it stands out easily.

Getting Videos onto Your iPod

Once you've downloaded some movies, TV shows, music videos, or podcasts, all you have to do to get them onto your iPod is connect it to your computer. iTunes will launch (if it's not already open) and automatically copy any videos you've downloaded onto your iPod (unless you've turned on the manual update feature—see the iTip below). It's as easy as that. By the way, movies are pretty large in file size, so depending on the size of your iPod, you might want to choose only certain movies or shows to be copied over, rather than all of them. To do this, click on your iPod in the Devices list on the left side of iTunes, then click on the Movies tab in the iPod Preferences. Turn on the check-box for **Sync Movies**, then below that, choose whether you want recent movies or unwatched movies from the pop-up menu, and turn on the checkboxes for any other movies you want copied to your iPod in the Movies section and in the Include Movies from Playlists section. Then, click the Apply button in the bottom-right corner of iTunes. Now do the same thing on both the TV Shows tab and Podcasts tab.

---

iTip: Manually Managing Videos

*Another way to control exactly which videos make it onto your iPod is to manage it manually. So, you literally drag-and-drop each movie, TV show, etc., you want right from your iTunes Library onto your iPod. To switch to manual mode, just go to the Summary tab, and turn on the checkbox for **Manually Manage Music and Videos**.*

Getting Home Movies to Play on Your iPod

Videos you download from the iTunes Store are already in the right format to play on your iPod, but if you import other videos into iTunes (like home movies or free videos you've downloaded from the Web), chances are they'll play within iTunes with no problem (iTunes supports most video formats), but not on your iPod (it doesn't support nearly as many). So, if you sync your iPod and get an error message along the lines of "This video cannot be played on your iPod," don't sweat it—you can have iTunes convert that video to a video file format your iPod does support by first clicking on the video in question, then going under the Advanced menu and choosing **Create iPod or iPhone Version**. That's it—it converts the video to a format your iPod supports, and now all you have to do is sync again, and the video is copied onto your iPod.

---

iTip: Getting Your Own Videos to Play in iTunes and on Your iPod

*Now, if your home movie isn't in a format that will play in iTunes, once it's downloaded onto your computer, you'll have to open it in QuickTime 7 Pro (if you don't have it, it's available at Apple.com for both PC and Mac) or QuickTime X in Snow Leopard (on a Mac). Once it's open in QuickTime Pro, go under the File menu and choose Export. In the Export dialog, for your export method, choose **Movie to iPod** from the pop-up menu, then hit the Save button, and the converted movie file will appear on your computer. Import it into iTunes, then connect your iPod and sync up. That's it!*

Watching iPod Videos on Your TV

All you need is Apple's Composite or Component AV cable (available from Apple.com or your local Apple Store), which connects your iPod to your TV. It's simple to use—connect the Dock connector to your iPod or Apple Universal Dock, then plug the video and audio cables into the AV jacks on your TV. Lastly, plug the USB cable into a USB Power Adapter or your computer. Now, go to your iPod's Videos menu, scroll down to Settings, and press the Center button. Choose **TV Out** and press the Center button to change the setting from Off to On, so that when you play your video on your iPod, it will play on your TV, as well, at full size (by the way, the video looks great—nearly DVD quality). If you use the Dock, it comes with a wireless remote, so you can sit back and run the whole thing from your couch. Sweet! *Note:* To play videos on your iPod while it's connected to your computer, turn off the Enable Disk Use checkbox on the Preferences Summary tab.

---

iTip: Importing Other Types of Video

*You can watch videos that aren't from the iTunes Store (your home movies, for example) as long as they're in either MPEG-4 or H.264 format (luckily, these are two very popular formats for digital video). Just open iTunes, find those videos on your computer, then drag-and-drop them onto the iTunes main window, and they'll be imported into iTunes. If that doesn't work, just go under the File menu and choose **Add to Library (PC: Add File to Library)**. You'll find these newly imported videos by clicking on the Movies link in the Source list on the left.*

Video Podcasts Aren't Under Videos on Your iPod

Your iPod treats video podcasts differently than movies, TV shows, and music videos in that video podcasts don't show up under the Videos menu. Instead, they have their own separate heading in the main menu. So, to see a video podcast, start at the main menu and choose **Podcasts**. This brings up a list of the different podcasts you've downloaded, and if you see a tiny TV screen icon below a podcast's name, that lets you know it's a video podcast. (By the way, I'm the co-host of a weekly video podcast called *Photoshop User TV*, with my buddies Dave Cross and Matt Kloskowski, where we share our favorite Adobe Photoshop tutorials and tips. We started this video podcast back in October 2005. You can watch it right on our website at www.photoshopusertv .com, or by subscribing to it for free from the iTunes Store. Just search for "Photoshop User TV.")

---

iTip: Putting Music Videos Where They Belong

If you've downloaded some MP4 music videos from the Web, you can drag-and-drop them into iTunes, but they won't show up under Music Videos. iTunes will list them under Movies, but it doesn't have to be that way. Go to your Movies Library, click on your imported music video, then press **Command-I (PC: Ctrl-I)** *to bring up its Get Info dialog. Click on the Options tab, and in the* **Media Kind pop-up menu***, choose* **Music Video***, then click OK, and now it will appear in your Music Videos smart playlist and Music Library.*

Moving Your Movies to Another Computer

If you want to move movies and other videos from one computer to another (you're allowed to authorize up to five computers to play your purchased video and music content from the iTunes Store—connect your iPod to another computer, click on it in the Source list, then choose **Authorize Computer** from the Store menu), just download the movies right from your iPod onto your other computer. Here's how: First, connect your iPod to the other computer you've authorized to play your music and videos. A dialog will appear asking you if you want to transfer your purchased videos and music to this other authorized computer (by the way, if it doesn't ask you, you can still have it do this by going under the File menu and choosing **Transfer Purchases from [your iPod's name]**). When you click OK, it takes over the task and copies your purchased videos and music onto the computer. Couldn't be easier or faster.

---

iTip: Stretching Your Battery Life When Watching Movies

*The thing that eats up the most battery power is that gloriously bright full-color screen. So, if you're watching a three-hour movie, and want to make sure you make it to the end without having to recharge (like when you're on a commercial flight), simply press the Center button three times to bring up the **Brightness slider**, then glide your finger counterclockwise around the Click Wheel to lower the brightness and extend your battery life (the darker you go, the longer your battery will last).*

Shooting Video on Your iPod nano

As hard as it is to believe, if you have an iPod nano, it actually has a very cool built-in video camera and audio microphone (I know. Amazing!). To shoot video, from the main menu, choose **Video Camera**, and you'll see a live preview of what you're pointing the back of the camera at. You can shoot video either wide (with the nano on its side, as shown above) or tall (for a cropped view). To start recording, just press the Center button (on the Click Wheel) and a red recording light starts blinking up in the right corner, and a timer starts to show how long you've been recording (if the screen is blank, your finger is probably covering the camera—don't feel bad, it's really easy to cover it without realizing it). To stop recording, just press the Center button again and your video is saved to your Camera Roll. To see your video, press the Menu button, and it shows you all the clips you've shot (in folders by date), when you shot them, and how long each clip runs. To play a video, choose it, then press the Play/Pause button on the Click Wheel. To pause or stop the video, press the same button. To delete a video, choose the video, then press-and-hold the Center button and a menu appears where you can scroll to Delete, then press the Center button to actually delete it.

---

iTip: Not Covering the Camera with Your Fingers

To keep from covering the video camera with your fingers, just hold your iPod nano by the side edges. You'll still have a finger free to start/stop shooting your video.

Adding Effects to Your Videos on Your iPod nano

Before you start shooting your video, you can apply some special effects, like Black & White, Sepia, X-Ray (I can't imagine why), Cyborg (cooler than you'd think), Film Grain, Thermal, Security Cam, and then some that get downright…well…let's just say you'd probably only apply these to videos of people you don't like (stuff like Bulge, Kaleido, Motion Blur, Mirror, Light Tunnel, Dent, Stretch, and Twirl). The thing to keep in mind is you have to choose an effect *before* you start shooting—you don't get to add these after. To bring up the list of effects, first choose **Video Camera** from the main menu, then press-and-hold the Center button until they appear onscreen. Use the Click Wheel to look at a live preview of the different effects. When you find one you want, select it and press the Center button. Now, you're ready to start filming, and that effect will be applied to your video (but only for this one video. If you want to use that effect again on the next video, you have to press-and-hold the Center button again, scroll to it, and select it again).

Transferring Your iPod nano Videos to Your Computer

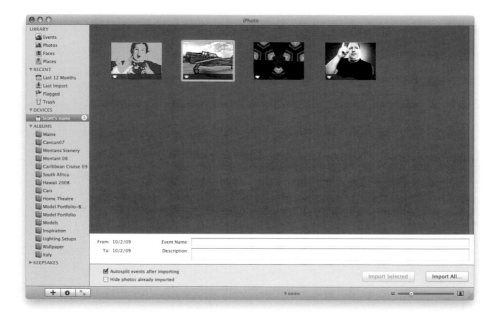

If you've got a Mac, you can use Apple's iPhoto (it came with your Mac) to transfer the videos you shot with your iPod nano to your Mac. Plug your iPod nano into your computer, and in iTunes, click on it under Devices on the left side. On the Summary tab, make sure the checkbox for **Enable Disk Use** is turned on, then click on the Photos tab, make sure the **Sync Photos From** checkbox is turned on and that iPhoto is selected in the pop-up menu, and then turn on the **Include Videos** checkbox. When you click the Sync button at the bottom right, your videos are imported into iPhoto. Easy enough. If you have a Windows PC, after you connect your iPod nano to your computer, in iTunes, click on it under Devices on the left side, then turn on the checkbox for Enable Disk Use (if you didn't already have it on). This mounts your iPod on your desktop just like it was a hard disk, so now you can go straight to the folder called "DCIM," and inside that folder, you'll find your videos—just drag-and-drop them right onto your PC. Easy enough.

---

iTip: Playing Videos Larger

*If you'd always like to have any videos you watch within iTunes play in the much larger floating video window, then go to the iTunes Preferences, click on Playback up top, and for **Play Movies and TV Shows** and **Play Music Videos**, choose **In a Separate Window** from the pop-up menus. If you always want your videos to play full screen, you can choose that from the pop-up menus, as well. Ahh, that's better.*

Chapter Five

Get the Freeze-Frame

Using Your iPod's Photo Features

So, does this chapter win the award for "Most Obvious Chapter Title" or what? It's almost too obvious a name for a chapter about working with photos on your iPod, but I used it anyway, because besides being too obvious, it's also too perfect. By the way (*Warning:* Quick iPod history lesson coming), there was a time when iPods only played music. In fact, for a while there was only one model of iPod that even supported the viewing of photos. It was called (are you ready for this) the "iPod photo." Its name was almost as obvious as the name of this chapter. Now, why does all this matter? It matters plenty, because although book editors don't read the introductions of books anymore, they do read these chapter intros. These people are really picky, and insist on seeing things in these chapter intros like long words and punctuation. They also like it if I can work in a French word or two, because then they get to use their French dictionary and apparently they get some kind of kickback or bonus when that happens. Plus, they love to casually mention it in front of other editors: "I was working on Scott's book today, and I would have been done sooner, but I had to keep loading the French dictionary." The other editors all look at each other and go, "Oooooh. French!" So basically, I do it for them. They have so little, so if I toss in a long word here (like ostensively), and a French phrase there (like *Mon oreille est un bouton de porte*), then they'll let lots of other stuff slip by. Like this intro, for example.

Mac: Getting Photos on Your iPod

If you're a Mac user, there are two ways to get your photos from your computer onto your iPod: (1) You can use Apple's iPhoto application (which comes preinstalled on every Mac). You just drag-and-drop your photos on your computer into iPhoto, and then when you sync your iPod to your computer, those photos will automatically be copied onto your iPod. By default, it imports all your photos and albums (if you created any— they're kind of like playlists, but made up of photos instead of songs), but if you want to have just specific albums of photos copied over to your iPod, when it's connected to your computer, click on it in the Source list on the left, then click on the Photos tab. Turn on the **Sync Photos From checkbox**, click on the **Selected Albums, Events, and Faces, and Automatically Include radio button**, and in the Albums list below, turn on the checkbox beside each album you want copied onto your iPod. (2) The other method is to just import a folder full of photos onto your computer, then connect your iPod to it, click on your iPod in the Devices list in iTunes, then click on the Photos tab. At the top, from the Sync Photos From pop-up menu, select **Choose Folder**, then locate that folder of images on your computer, and click the Open button. (*Note:* If you create subfolders inside that main folder, they'll be imported into your iPod as separate albums, as if you were using iPhoto. Cool, eh?) Now, just click the Apply button in the bottom-right corner of iTunes and your images in that folder will be synced onto your iPod.

Windows PC: Getting Photos on Your iPod

If you're using a PC, there are two ways to get your photos from your computer onto your iPod: (1) Use Adobe Photoshop Elements (for around $80), which has a very robust photo organizer built right in, as well as amazing image-editing controls. When your photos are organized in Photoshop Elements, connect your iPod to your computer and, in iTunes, click on it in the Source list on the left. Then click on the Photos tab, turn on the **Sync Photos From checkbox**, and in its pop-up menu, **Photoshop Elements** should be selected. Just below that menu, you can choose whether you want to import every single photo and album you have or just specific albums (you'll need to have albums created in Elements to choose this option). Now, click the Apply button in the bottom-right corner. Or (2) you can just put your photos inside a folder on your computer. (*Note:* If you create subfolders inside your new folder, they'll be imported into your iPod as separate folders, just like with Elements' albums.) When your photos are in a folder, connect your iPod to your computer, and in iTunes, click on it in the Source list on the left, then click on the Photos tab. From the Sync Photos From pop-up menu, select **Choose Folder**, then choose the folder with your pictures, and click the OK button. Now just click the Apply button in the bottom-right corner of iTunes and your images in that folder will be synced to your iPod.

Viewing Photos You've Imported

Once you've synced your photos over onto your iPod, viewing them is easy. From the main menu, scroll down to **Photos**, then press the Center button. Any albums of photos you've imported will appear in a list. To see the photos in a particular album, scroll to that album, then press the Center button again and tiny thumbnails of the photos in that album will appear. Use the Click Wheel to move to the photo you want to see (you'll see a little yellow rectangle around the currently selected image), then press the Center button to see it at full-screen size. To see the next photo at full-screen size, press the Fast-Forward button. To see the previous photo, press the Rewind button. To scroll quickly through your images at full-screen size, just glide around the Click Wheel clockwise (to move quickly forward) or counterclockwise (to move quickly back to the beginning of that album). To get back to the thumbnails again, press the Menu button.

Seeing a Slide Show of Your Photos

To see a slide show of your photos (complete with some slick moving transitions), start at the main menu, scroll down, and click on **Photos**. Now click on the photo album you want to see as a slide show, and press the **Play/Pause button** to start it. To pause a running slide show, press the Play/Pause button again (to restart it, just press it once again). To return to your list of albums, press the Menu button. Also, if you're scrolling through your thumbnails, you can start a slide show from any thumbnail by just pressing the Play/Pause button, and your slide show will start with that photo.

---

iTip: Adding Music to Your Slide Show

*If there's one thing a slide show definitely needs, it's a music track playing behind it. You can add music in one of two ways: You can assign a song to an album in iPhoto, then that song plays automatically when you play that slide show on your iPod. If you'd prefer to choose your background music "on the fly," go to the iPod's main menu, click on Photos, click on Settings, then click on **Music**, and select which playlist you'd like to play during the slide show. Now you can start your slide show. Also, even though in iPhoto you can pick either a single song or a playlist, in the iPod, you can only pick a playlist. The only way to get a single song in the iPod is to create a playlist that only has one song in it.*

Customizing Your Slide Show

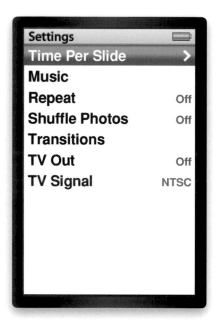

Your iPod gives you a surprising amount of control over how (and where) your slide show is displayed. To find these controls, start at the main menu, scroll down and click on Photos, then scroll down and click on **Settings** for a list of slide show options. By default, each slide will remain on your iPod screen for five seconds on an iPod nano, or three seconds on an iPod classic, but you can set it so each photo remains onscreen longer (or shorter, if you like) by clicking on Time Per Slide and then choosing from the list of times (in seconds). You can also choose to have your slide show repeat when it gets to the end by turning on Repeat, and you can see random photos by turning on Shuffle Photos. The Transitions preference lets you choose what happens between slides to reveal the next slide (the iPod nano and the iPod classic have different transitions available). Personally, I like the Dissolve effect on the iPod nano, but you can choose any one you'd like. If you want a "cut" (one slide replaces the other with no transition between them), choose None. If you want to show your slide show on TV (you're using Apple's Composite or Component AV Cable to connect your iPod to your television—see the next page), once you've connected your iPod to your TV's video and audio jacks, scroll down to TV Out, press the Center button, and set it to On or Ask. Now, press Menu to jump back to your list of albums, click on the one you want to see as a slide show, then press the Play/Pause button.

Seeing Your Slide Show on TV

To see your slide show on a TV, use the Apple Composite or Component AV Cable (available from Apple.com or your local Apple Store) to connect your iPod to your TV. Just connect the Dock connector to your iPod or Apple Universal Dock, then insert the audio and video connectors into the input jacks on your TV. Once connected, from the main menu, click on Photos, then scroll down and click on Settings. Scroll to **TV Out** and click the Center button until it changes to Ask. Now, click on the Menu button and scroll to the photo album you want to display as a slide show, then press the Center button, scroll to the photo you want to start with, and press the Center button, once again. Once your full-screen image appears, press the Center button to bring up the screen shown above, and use the Click Wheel to move the blue button to Yes on an iPod nano, or On on an iPod classic, which sets your iPod to display on a TV (just be sure you've connected your iPod to your TV before turning this on). Now press the Center button one more time to begin your "big screen" experience.

Getting Your Stored Photos onto Your Computer

If you've been using your iPod like a hard disk or USB device and have backed up a bunch of photos (or other files) onto it, and now you want to transfer them to another computer so you can edit them, sort them, and if you like, transfer them from that computer back to your iPod, here's how to do just that: Connect your iPod to your computer, then when iTunes launches, click on your iPod in the Source list on the left side of the window. On the Summary tab, in the Options section, turn on the checkbox for **Enable Disk Use**. Once you do this, your iPod will appear on your computer as a mounted disk. Go to your computer's desktop, double-click on the iPod icon, and you'll see the folder with your stored photos (just don't disturb the folder named "Photos"). Now you can select these photos and drag them onto your computer.

---

iTip: Using Your iPod for Business Presentations

Want to really "tune up" the crowd at your next business presentation? Instead of lugging your laptop to the conference room, just bring along your iPod and Apple's Composite or Component AV Cable, and connect your iPod directly to the projector. Instead of showing photos, show a playlist of the slides you want to use in your presentation. Click the iPod's Fast-Forward button to advance to the next "slide" (you can even have music behind your slide presentation—see the iTip on page 71). Also, while in slide show mode, you can see your next photo on the iPod screen before it appears on the projection screen. If you really want to take things up a notch, use Apple's Wireless Remote, so you can stand at the front of the room and advance through your slides.

Chapter Six

iTouch Myself
Using Your iPod touch

Before we get started, I just want you to know that I'm fully aware that: (a) the real name of the song by The DiVinyls is "I Touch Myself" and not "iTouch Myself," but it just seemed so obvious a tie-in that I had to do it; and (b) I know that the title is a little naughty, but as any book publisher will tell you, working naughty things into your book is really what ultimately sells the book. It's not the step-by-step instructions or helpful tips that make your life easier. As my editor says, "That stuff is for suckers." In fact, oftentimes I'll submit a chapter, and my editor will call me (we'll call him "Ted" because that's his real name), and Ted will say something along the lines of "Do you want this book to sell? Then you'd better 'sex it up' a bit." So I go back to those chapters and I try to insert what I believe to be totally innocent words, but for which people with naughty minds (not you) apparently insert their own meanings. Now, because you're not one of these people, you totally won't get how these words could possibly be misconstrued as "dirty," but rest assured, "those" people will find a way. Here's a perfect example: melons. See, it's just a fruit commonly sold at every grocery store, but "those" people assign some sort of twisted meaning to it. Pickle. See, another innocent grocery store item (much like sausage or wiener), but Ted insists I put these in, including the occasional lurid poultry reference, like thighs and breasts (I don't know about you, but I'm getting hungry). I'm sorry you had to be exposed to this seamy underbelly of publishing, but I thought you'd rather hear it from me, instead of picking it up on the streets.

Turning Your iPod touch On and Off

To turn your iPod touch on, just press-and-hold the **Sleep/Wake button** located on the top. The Apple logo will appear for a few moments, and then you'll see the Home screen. To put it to sleep (which is a great way to conserve battery life when you're not using it), you just press that same Sleep/Wake button once (when you put it to sleep, you'll hear a little click sound and your screen will go black). To wake it from sleep, you can either press that Sleep/Wake button again or press the Home button on the bottom center (just below the touchscreen). When it wakes, the screen is still locked (just in case you awakened it accidentally), so to unlock it, just press your finger on the gray arrow button onscreen, slide it to the right, and the Home screen appears. To turn your iPod touch completely off, just press-and-hold the Sleep/Wake button for a few seconds until the red Slide to Power Off button appears, then take your finger, press lightly on it, and just slide it to the right. Your screen will turn black, you'll see a small round status icon for just a moment, and then your iPod touch will power off.

---

iTip: Two Ways to Adjust the Volume

You can turn the volume up/down without having to look at or touch the screen by using the button on the left side of the iPod touch. You can also adjust the volume onscreen with the volume slider while playing a song or video.

Using the Home Screen

The Home screen is the launching point for all of your iPod touch's features. In fact, this Home screen is so important that there's only one "real" button on the front of your iPod touch (found just below the touchscreen, and circled above in red). Anytime you press that button, it takes you right to the Home screen. Once you're at the Home screen, the icons you see on it are actually some of the different applications that come with your iPod touch (like the Safari Web browser, a calendar application, a contacts application, etc.), and there's a Settings icon to access your preferences. To use any one of these applications (called apps), just tap your finger once on the icon for that app. For example, if you wanted to look for some music, you'd just tap once on the Music icon to enter the Music app of your iPod touch.

Rearranging Your Home Screen Icons

If you want to rearrange the order of your apps on the Home screen, just tap-and-hold on any one of the application icons for a few seconds. All your icons will start wiggling, and that means you can now just drag them around in the order you want them. Once you're satisfied with your new arrangement, just press the Home button to lock them in place. If you want to move an icon to another screen (you can have up to 11 Home screens), once they're wiggling, tap-and-hold on the icon, and drag it off the right side. Also, if your first Home screen is full, and you download another app, your iPod will automatically create a new Home screen for it. You can change screens by just flicking with your finger (left to right and vice versa) on the screen. You can rearrange apps in iTunes, as well. Once you've chosen the apps to sync on the Applications tab in the iPod Preferences, an image of each Home screen will appear. You can click-and-drag the apps from one Home screen to another right on these images.

---

iTip: How Many Home Screens Do You Have?

When you have two or more Home screens, you'll see two or more little dots (one white, and the rest gray) appear below the fourth row of icons. That lets you know how many Home screens you have and which one you're currently on (so if you see four dots, and the third one is "lit" [white], you're on the third screen). To switch between them, just flick the screens left or right with your finger.

What Double-Clicking the Home Button Does

Actually, you get to decide what it does by going to the Home screen, tapping on **Settings**, then tapping on **General**, and tapping on **Home**. You'll see a list of what you can assign a double-click of the Home button to do. For example, if you find yourself using the Search feature a lot, tap on Search, and now with just a quick double-click, you're ready to do a search (no more having to go back to the Home screen first). Whatever you see in this list that you wind up digging around for the most should be assigned to be just a double-click away.

---

iTip: The Fastest Way to Get Back to the First Home Screen

*Once you've got a bunch of different Home screens, it can take quite a few swipes to get you back to the first Home screen, so instead, you can use this shortcut: when you're on one of the other screens, just press the **Home button** once (the hard button on the front, below the touchscreen), and it jumps you directly to the first Home screen.*

Playing a Song

To play a song, from the Home screen, tap on **Music**, then tap on **Songs** along the bottom of the screen. Scroll to the song you want (by "flicking" upward on the touchscreen), then just tap on the song you want to hear—it will start playing and you'll see the cover art full screen (as shown above). At the bottom of the screen are four controls: a Rewind button (the left-facing arrows), a Play/Pause button (in the center), and a Fast-Forward button (the right-facing arrows). There's also a volume slider—just slide the little knob to the right with your finger to increase the volume (or left to lower it). To fast forward through your song, press-and-hold the Fast-Forward button. To jump to the next song in the list, just tap the Fast-Forward button once (the Rewind button works the same way to go back in your song or in the list).

---

iTip: When There's No Cover Art

If you choose to play a song that doesn't have its own cover art, your iPod substitutes a fake cover with a large musical note (actually, it's a couple of eighth notes), which really makes you appreciate cover art.

Scrubbing, Repeating, and Shuffling

Once a song is playing, you can scrub through it by tapping on the center of the screen, and a scrubby slider will appear near the top. Use your finger to drag the little round knob forward or backward. Also, you can adjust the speed of the scrubby slider by dragging your finger straight down while you're scrubbing—the lower you drag your finger, the slower the scrubbing goes (it's okay if it slips off the little round knob, it will still scrub). (*Note:* This is a great tool if you're trying to figure out the words to a song. As soon as a lyric goes by, you can scrub back just a little bit and hear it again, and repeat that as many times as you'd like until you realize it's saying "'scuse me while I kiss the sky" instead of "'scuse me while I kiss this guy.") There are two other controls that appear just below each end of this scrubby slider: (1) On the left is the **Repeat icon**. If you tap on it once, it turns blue (to let you know repeat is turned on), and it will repeat your current playlist of songs. If you tap it again, a tiny "1" appears on the icon, letting you know that it will now repeat just the current song again and again until you turn it off by tapping it once more. And, (2) on the right side is the **Shuffle icon**. Tap once to turn it on, and it shuffles the songs currently chosen (playing them in a random order). Tap it again to turn Shuffle off. Tap the center of the screen again to hide these controls. By the way, while you're playing a song, after just a few seconds, your iPod's screen goes to sleep to help save battery life. To reawaken it, just press the Home button, and then slide the unlock button to the right.

Seeing the Other Songs on an Album

When you play a song, if the song has album art, it appears full screen (if not, you'll just see a large musical note). If you want to see the other songs you've downloaded from that same album, just tap twice (quickly) on the center of the screen, and a list of other songs appears (if you only see one song listed, you have only downloaded one song from that album). The listing includes each song's length and any star ratings you've applied to them (as seen above). To play one of these songs, just tap on it. To hear the album's next song, tap the Fast-Forward button, and it skips to the next song. To return to the normal Cover Art view, just tap the little Cover Art button in the top right of the screen. To return to the regular Songs list (or the Playlists, Artists, or Albums list you were in), tap the back arrow button in the top-left corner of the screen.

---

iTip: Hearing All the Songs from All of an Artist's Albums

*Let's say you like Aerosmith—you probably have lots of their songs from all different albums. Here's how to hear them all (without having to make a special playlist or navigate from album to album): On the Home screen, tap on **Music**, then tap on **Artists**, then find Aerosmith. It will list all the albums that you have songs from, and if you tap on an album to play those songs, when it's done, it stops. However, at the top, you'll see **All Songs**. Tap on that, then tap on the first song to start it playing, and it plays all their songs, no matter which album they're from (well, at least from the ones you downloaded).*

Getting to Your Playlists

The playlists you create in iTunes are copied over to your iPod touch when you connect it to your computer (this is called "syncing"). To play the songs in your synced
playlists, tap on the **Music icon** (from the Home screen), then tap once on **Playlists**
at the bottom of the screen. This brings up your list of playlists (for more on playlists, see
Chapter 8). To see the songs in a playlist, just tap on it. To hear any song, tap on it and it
starts playing. The rest of the songs that follow in that playlist will now play in order.

---

iTip: Shuffling Your Playlist

*At the very top of each playlist is the **Shuffle** option. Tap on it, and it immediately starts
playing that playlist in a random order.*

Making On–The–Go Playlists

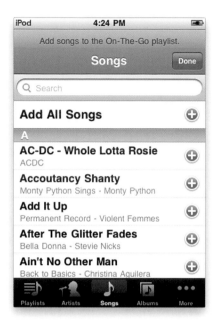

You can create an instant playlist right from your iPod. It's called an "On-The-Go" playlist, and to create one, start by tapping once on the **Music icon**, then tap on **Playlists**, and near the top of the list of playlists, you'll see **On-The-Go**. Tap on On-The-Go once, and a list of your songs will appear. You'll see a + (plus sign) button to the right of each song (as seen above), which you tap to add that song to your On-The-Go playlist. When you're done, tap the Done button in the upper-right corner. Now when you tap On-The-Go in the Playlists list, it will display those songs. To add more songs, tap the Edit button in the top-right corner, then tap the + button in the top left, and that list of all your songs (with the plus sign beside them) will appear again—just tap the + button beside any songs you want to add, then tap the Done button (if the plus sign is grayed out, it means that song is already in your On-The-Go playlist).

Creating Genius Playlists

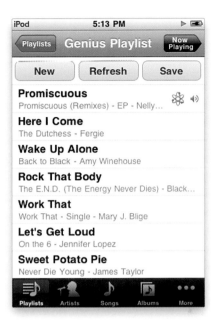

If you're working out, and this really great track comes on, and it really gets you totally pumped, and you think to yourself, "I wish I had a playlist of more stuff like this," you can have your iPod automatically search through your songs and create a playlist based on that track you're listening to—just tap on the album cover of the song and then tap on the atom icon that appears near the top. Of course, you don't have to have a song playing to make a Genius playlist. Just tap on the **Playlists button** in the Music app, then tap on **Genius** up at the top of the list, and it will bring up your iPod's song list. If, for example, you tapped on "Promiscuous" by Nelly Furtado, it would make a 25-song playlist, which on my iPod would includes songs like: "Here I Come" by Fergie, "Rock That Body" by Black Eyed Peas, "Work That" by Mary J. Blige, "Let's Get Loud" by Jennifer Lopez, and so on. By the way, once it's created a Genius playlist for you, it starts playing it right away, but if you tap the Back arrow at the top left, it'll not only display the songs in the Genius playlist, but it'll display three buttons across the top: tap New to create a totally new Genius playlist based on a different song; tap Refresh if you don't like the playlist it created and you want it to try again; and if you love that playlist and want to save it, tap Save. (*Note:* In order to use this feature, you must have the Genius feature turned on in iTunes on your computer. Once you sync your iPod touch to your computer with the Genius feature enabled, you'll be able to create Genius playlists directly on your iPod.)

Using the Automatic Genius Mix

This is one of those features I personally just love, because what a Genius mix does is look at your existing Music Library, and create playlists of songs that go together, and it does all of this without requiring any input from you (you can read more about these in Chapter 8). Here, I'm going to show you how to set it up to work on your iPod touch: The first step actually starts in iTunes on your computer, so open iTunes then go under the Store menu and choose **Update Genius**. (If you don't already have it on, you'll have to turn Genius on first on the same menu.) Now, when you connect your iPod touch to your computer, if it is set to sync with your entire Music Library, your Genius mixes will be added to your iPod. If you have your iPod set to sync only checked songs and videos, you'll need to go to the Music tab in the iPod Preferences and turn on the Genius Mixes checkbox, and if you manually manage your music, you'll have to drag-and-drop the Genius mixes in the Source list on the left onto your iPod. To get to your Genius mixes on your iPod touch, from the Home screen, tap on **Music**. If you look along the bottom, there's a new Genius button on the far left, next to Playlists. Tap on **Genius**, and your first Genius mix will appear with a Play icon in the center of the album covers. Tap on that icon to start playing this mix. The little dots below the album covers tell you how many Genius mixes you have (just like your multiple Home screens, the white dot is the active screen). Swipe your finger on the screen to the left or right to move between Genius mixes.

Searching for Songs Already on Your iPod

If you've got hundreds, or even thousands, of songs on your iPod, you're gonna love the built-in search feature (you just have to know where to find it, because it's not that obvious at first). For example, if you want to search your song list, from the Home screen, tap on **Music**, then tap on **Songs** (at the bottom of the screen), then "flick" downward (from top to bottom) right on the screen, and a search field appears at the top. Tap in it, and start typing in the name of a song, artist, or album, and as soon as you type just a few letters, the results start appearing onscreen. Although there is the "iPod touch–wide" Spotlight search feature (which you get to by flicking to the right from the Home screen) that searches everything on your iPod touch (including email, contacts, etc.), by going to the Music app first and tapping on Songs, it just searches your song list, so it's easier to get right to the song you want.

---

iTip: Playing Audiobooks

Like any other iPod, the iPod touch can play audiobooks you've downloaded, and one nice feature (mentioned earlier in the book) is that if you listen to your audiobook on your iPod, when you sync it with your computer, it tells iTunes the exact spot where you paused, so you can pick up listening to the book on your computer. If you pause the book in iTunes, when you re-sync your iPod touch, it tells your touch where you left off.

Visual Searching by Album Cover

The iPod touch has the same Cover Flow view that iTunes itself has, where you can visually scroll through your entire music collection by cover art. To do this, just turn your iPod touch sideways (so the screen is horizontal), and it automatically enters the **Cover Flow view**. To move through the covers, just swipe your finger horizontally across the screen and the covers flow by in the direction you're "flicking." To view the songs on an album, just tap on it and the cover flips over to show you the songs you've downloaded from that album. Tap on any song to play it. To return to the Cover Flow view, just tap twice in the center of the screen (your music doesn't stop playing—the view just changes back to Cover Flow).

---

iTip: Redeeming Gift Cards from Your iPod touch

*If you've got an iTunes gift card or a promo code (like Pepsi offered during one special promotion), you can redeem these right from your iPod touch: Just tap on **iTunes** on the Home screen, then tap on **Music** at the bottom left, tap on **New Releases** at the top left of the Music screen, and scroll down to the bottom of the list. Tap on **Redeem**, enter your gift card, gift certificate, or promo code, and the amount is added to your account.*

Controlling Your iPod While in Another App

Once you start a song or playlist going, you can leave the Music app by clicking the Home button. The music will keep playing and you can then launch another app, such as the Weather app. However, if you want to control your music while you're in another app, you don't have to go back to the Music app to do so. All you have to do is double-click the Home button. This will bring up some onscreen controls and overlay them on top of the app you're currently in. Once the controls appear, you can pause the song, advance to the next one, go back to the previous one, control the volume, or tap the Music button to return to the Music app. Once you're done with the controls, you can just tap the Close button to return to the app you were in. Also note that the default behavior for double-clicking the Home button is to take you to your Home screen. However, if you have music playing, it brings up these controls instead.

---

iTip: Use the Volume Button When in Another App

If all you want to do is control the volume, you don't have to bring up the Music controls. You can use the button on the left side of the iPod touch to control your volume while a song is playing.

Changing the Buttons at the Bottom of the Music App

At the bottom of the main iPod touch Music screen is a navigation bar that, by default, gives you one-tap access to your Playlists, Artists, Songs, and Albums (or Genius mixes, if you have that feature turned on), and there's a More button to take you to other areas within your Music app. You can customize this little navigation bar so your favorite places are there (for example, you could replace Artists with Podcasts, so you're just one tap away from your list of podcasts). To do that, tap once on the **More button**, then when the More screen appears, tap the dark blue **Edit button** in the top-left corner of the screen. This shows you all the buttons you can choose from. Press-and-hold on the one you want to move to the bottom, and slide it right down to the spot you want it, then remove your finger, and the button is replaced. You're basically dragging-and-dropping buttons. (You can also reorder them the same way.)

---

iTip: You Can't Replace the More Button

The one button it won't let you replace is the More button, because if you were to replace it, you wouldn't be able to get back to that Configure screen again, or any of the other buttons that aren't visible, for that matter.

Finding Stuff in the iTunes Store

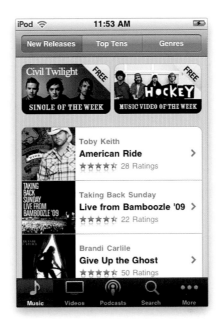

If you've got a Wi-Fi connection, you can log into the iTunes Store to buy music, movies, apps, etc., and have them downloaded onto your iPod touch right there on the spot. Here's how it works: From the Home Screen, tap on the purple **iTunes icon**. When you enter the iTunes Store, there are navigation buttons along the bottom of the screen to help you get to what you're looking for, and three shortcut buttons appear along the top of the screen. Probably the most used button is Search (on the bottom)—tap on it and the keyboard appears, so you can type in the name of the song, artist, movie, etc., you want to search for. To preview any audio or video file, just tap on it. Prices are listed with each song, video, etc., and if you tap on a price, it changes into a green Buy Now button. If you tap on Buy Now, it's going to ask you for your iTunes account password (to make sure someone else isn't making buying decisions for you), and then whatever you bought downloads onto your iPod touch. You can find newly downloaded songs in the Music app, under Playlists, in the Purchased playlist.

---

iTip: It Doesn't Matter Whether You Buy on Your iPod or Your Computer

When you get back to your computer and sync your iPod touch, anything you bought is automatically uploaded to your computer to keep everything in sync.

Downloading Audio and Video Podcasts

Podcasts are short audio or video shows, usually on a particular topic, and luckily the vast majority of them are absolutely free, and if you've got a Wi-Fi connection, you can download and watch them right on your iPod touch (otherwise, you can download them in iTunes on your computer and sync them to your iPod touch). To find podcasts on your iPod touch, tap **iTunes** on the Home screen, then tap **Podcasts** at the bottom of the screen. This brings up a list of podcasts, and you can look at What's Hot, the Top Tens (in a variety of categories), or a full list of Categories. Once you find one you want to download, tap on it to watch it stream to your iPod, or tap the Free button to the right of it, and Free changes to Download to download the entire episode (that way, you can watch it without having an active Internet connection, like when you're on a flight). Tap it to download that podcast. *Note:* If it's a video podcast, you'll see a little TV monitor icon to the left of the Free button.

---

iTip: Scott's Video Podcasts

*I co-host two weekly video podcasts: One is called **Photoshop User TV** (www.photo-shopusertv.com) and the other is called **The Shoot** (it's a show that teaches digital pho-tography techniques), and you can subscribe to these podcasts for free right from within iTunes on your computer, or download them right from your iPod touch.*

Watching Videos

If you've downloaded any videos (movies, TV shows, etc.), you can watch them by starting at the Home screen, and tapping once on **Videos**, which brings up the main Videos menu. All your videos are organized into categories (Movies, TV Shows, Music Videos, and Podcasts). To watch a video, tap on it and it begins playing. Videos play horizontally (so you have a wider view), so turn your iPod touch sideways. Once it's playing, to see the controls for pausing, fast forwarding, rewinding, and volume, just tap anywhere on the screen and they appear near the bottom. A scrubber bar also appears at the top of the screen—just drag the knob to the right to scrub forward in your video or drag left to scrub backward.

---

iTip: Toggling Between Video Modes

The iPod touch has two video modes: Cinematic, which displays your video in a wide-screen view more like the original theatrical presentation, so you'll see your video in "letterbox" view with thin black bars at the top and bottom of the screen. There's also Full Screen view, which zooms in, so your video fills the screen. To toggle between these two modes, just tap twice on the screen.

Deleting Videos

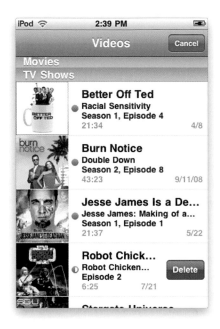

Your iPod touch is the only iPod that lets you actually delete something (in this case, a video) from right within the iPod itself (normally, you can only delete songs, videos, photos, etc., within iTunes on your computer, and then when you sync, it removes that same item from your iPod). To delete a video from your iPod touch, take your finger, press it on one side of the video listing, and drag it toward the other side (right-to-left or left-to-right). You'll see a red **Delete button** appear on the right side—just tap on it and the video gets deleted.

---

iTip: Using Parental Controls to Protect Your Kids

*The parental controls allow you to keep your kids from downloading inappropriate movies, apps, or songs—you get to choose the ratings of the movies they can download, whether they can download songs with Explicit lyrics or not, etc. To turn these on (and choose your options and a password, so they can't disable them), start at the Home screen, tap on **Settings**, then tap on **General**, and tap on **Restrictions**. Now tap on Enable Restrictions at the top, and a list of things you can restrict appears below it (by default, it restricts everything). To turn off a restriction, just tap on it. Scroll down further for a list of Allowed Content options.*

Renting Movies

If you've got a Wi-Fi Internet connection, you can rent movies right from your iPod touch. On the Home screen, just tap on **iTunes** to connect to the iTunes Store, then tap on **Videos**. Tap on the movie you want, and if it's available for rental, you'll see a **Rent Movie button** and the price. At the time of this writing, it's $2.99 for a 24-hour rental ($3.99 for an HD rental), however, that 24-hour period doesn't start until you actually start watching the movie, and you can watch it as many times as you want within that 24-hour period. After the 24 hours is up, the movie will automatically be deleted from your iPod touch. Also, you do have 30 days to start watching your rented movie, but again, the 24-hour clock doesn't start until you start the movie.

---

iTip: Moving Rented Movies from Your Computer to Your iPod touch

*iTunes movie rentals aren't automatically synced to your iPod touch—you have to select them and manually sync them. To do this, connect your iPod touch to your computer and select it in the Source list on the left. You'll see your rented movies in the Movies tab in the main iTunes window. Click on the **Move button** next to each rented movie you want on your iPod touch, then click the Apply button at the bottom right. Also, your computer needs to be connected to the Internet at the time you do the sync. Once you sync your rental(s) to your iPod, it is removed from your computer's iTunes Movies Library.*

Connect Your iPod touch to Your TV

You can watch your movies, TV shows, podcasts, and music videos on the big screen—all you need is either the Apple Component AV Cable or the Apple Composite AV Cable (see Chapter 4). The Apple Composite AV Cable is for connecting to TVs (or projectors) with standard RCA-style connectors—yellow for video, and red and white for stereo audio. However, if you have a newer TV (or HD projector), chances are it has component jacks on the back, which would be red, green, and blue, as well as red and white stereo inputs. So, make sure you check out your TV to see which connections it has before buying your cable. Also note that included with these cables is an additional AC-to-USB adapter, so you'll have power to your iPod touch while it's playing. This way you can just leave the cable connected to your TV at all times if you like. Once you have the cable, just tap **Settings** from your iPod's Home screen and then tap **Video**. Under the **TV Out options**, you can have the iPod display the appropriate format by turning Widescreen on, if you have a 16:9 widescreen TV, and choose between NTSC (U.S.) or PAL (Europe). When you're done, press the Home button, and then tap on Videos, and find the video you want to watch. Connect the cable to your TV and iPod touch, and make sure your TV is on the appropriate input for either your composite or component connection. Now start your video and you'll see it on the big screen. Also, while your video is playing, your iPod serves as a remote that allows you to pause, skip chapters, etc.

Downloading Apps

If there's one thing that really makes people fall head-over-heels in love with their iPod touch, it's the downloadable apps from the iTunes Store. (By the way, there are over 85,500 apps there already, and it's growing so fast that by the time you read this, it'll probably be around 100,000.) What's perhaps most amazing is that an incredible amount of these apps are absolutely free, but don't let that throw you—the quality of many of them is astounding! The ones that do charge average anywhere from 99¢ to around $2.99, with some a bit more, but even most pay-for apps are less than $4.99. If you have a Wi-Fi connection, you can tap the **App Store icon** on your iPod touch's Home Screen (or you can shop from iTunes on your computer) and start browsing. Once you find an app you want, you can tap the word Free (if it's free), or tap the price button, and you'll get the option to Install/Buy the app. Either way, you'll be prompted for your iTunes Store password. Once you enter your password, the app will begin to download and install right on your iPod touch, so it's just one tap away.

---

iTip: Where to Find "Killer" Apps

My buddy, and Tech Editor of this book, Terry White is an absolute iPod touch guru, and finds the slickest apps and features. He puts a new one each week (every Friday) on his blog called "Terry White's Tech Blog." Check it out at http://terrywhite.com/techblog/.

Deleting Apps

Although you can't delete the core set of iPod touch apps put there by Apple when you bought it, you can easily delete apps that you've downloaded from the App Store. From the Home screen, tap-and-hold your finger on the app you want to remove and all of your icons will start to wiggle. You'll see an X appear in the upper-left corner of each app you downloaded from the App store. Just tap the X to remove the app from your iPod touch. The next time you sync your iPod touch, the app will also be removed from iTunes.

---

iTip: Viewing Your iTunes Store Account Info

*If you want to view or change your iTunes Store account info, you can do that right from your iPod touch. From the Home screen, tap on **Settings**, then scroll down to **Store** and tap on it. Now tap on **View Account,** enter your iTunes user account password, then you'll have access to your account info, so you can change your payment method, or even sign up to receive the store newsletter.*

Getting New Features and Bug Fixes for Apps

If you see a little number appear alongside the icon for the App Store on your Home screen, that's just telling you how many updates have been released for the apps on your iPod touch. These updates from the apps' developers (which are usually free) include bug fixes, but often they also include improvements and brand new features, as well, so I always download these updates (when I have a Wi-Fi connection, of course). To get the updates, tap on the **App Store icon**, then tap on **Updates** at the bottom, and you'll see a list of your apps that have updates available. Tap on an app in the list, and it will tell you what's included in the update (along with any new features). To download that update, tap on the word "Free" and it begins to download. If you have a number of apps that need updates (I just checked and had five myself), you can update them all at once by tapping the **Update All button** on the Updates screen.

---

iTip: How to Have More Than 11 Screens of Apps

Okay, you can't actually have more than 11 Home screens, but you can actually have more apps than 11 Home screens can hold. In fact, you can have as many apps as you have memory available for, although you can only see icons for 180 apps. To find these other "hidden" apps, just use the Spotlight search feature (flick to the right from your first Home screen) and type in the name of the app you want.

Using the Built-In Keyboard

Anytime you need to type something on your iPod touch, a keyboard automatically appears onscreen. If the keys look kind of small, that's only because they are. Luckily, Apple added some features that make using the keyboard a lot easier. As you type onscreen, a large version of the letter you just typed pops up in front of your fingers, so you can see instantly if you hit the right letter. I can tell you from experience that the more you use this keyboard, the easier it gets, so if you wind up misspelling just about every word when you first start—don't sweat it—in just a couple of days you'll be misspelling only every third or fourth word. There's also a pretty clever auto-complete function. Although it will suggest a word while you're typing it, go ahead and finish the word (especially if you've spelled it wrong) and it will replace your misspelled word with the correct word (95% of the time). You do have to get used to typing a word, seeing that you've misspelled it, and continuing to type. If you do that—you'll be amazed at how quickly you'll be able to type using this keyboard.

---

iTip: Fixing Typos

If you need to go back and fix a typo that the auto-complete feature didn't catch, just press-and-hold approximately where the typo occurred, and a magnifying Loupe appears onscreen, so you can not only clearly see the location of your cursor, but you can move the cursor with your finger, as well, to quickly fix the mistake.

Getting a Much Larger Keyboard

If you want a much larger version of your iPod touch's keyboard, just turn it sideways (anytime the keyboard is visible) and you'll get the wide-screen version you see above (perfect if you have big fingers, or if you're not yet accustomed to the keyboard—it's a great place to practice your keyboard skills). This works for email, the Safari Web browser, and just about anywhere you need to use the keyboard.

---

iTip: Easy Access to Special Characters on Your Keyboard

If you need a special character, like an accent mark over a letter, just press–and–hold on the letter and a pop-up menu of hidden special characters will appear. Or, how about if you need an ellipse (that row of three little dots [like this...])? Just press–and–hold the Period key, and a menu pops up with it. Need Spanish punctuation marks? Press–and–hold on the ! or ? keys. Try the dollar sign ($) for international currency symbols. Press–and–hold the number 0 for the degrees symbol. There's a lot of hidden stuff, if you just press–and–hold.

Copying-and-Pasting Stuff

I say "stuff" because you can cut, copy, and paste more than text (though that's probably what you'll do the most). You can also copy-and-paste graphics. Here's how: First, find what you want to copy, press your finger on it for a second, then release (if it's text, press right on the word you want to copy for a second, or any one of the words, then let go). In a moment, a menu will pop up with **Select or Select All**, or just Copy (depending on what app you're in and where you're copying from). If you want one or more words, just tap Select. It will highlight the word you tapped on, but if you want other words to the left or right of it, just drag the little blue dot on either side of that word until all the words you want are highlighted (if you want all your text selected, then you'd have tapped Select All). Tap **Copy** from the menu that appears above your highlighted text. Now, just go where you want this text to appear, press-and-hold for just a second, then release. Tap **Paste** from the menu that appears above that spot, and it pastes your text in. Graphics work the same way—press-and-hold for a moment, then release, then tap Copy on the menu that pops up (you also have the choice to save the image here). Find where you want it to go, press-and-hold for a moment, then release, and choose Paste.

Getting Internet Access

When you want to jump on the Web, you need access to a wireless Internet connection (or a Wi-Fi network, for short). You find Wi-Fi networks at places like Starbucks, McDonald's, many hotel lobbies, etc., or you can jump on your office or home Wi-Fi network. When you tap on the **Safari icon** on the Home screen, your iPod touch immediately searches for an Internet connection, and if it sees a wireless network, it offers you the opportunity to try to access it. If it's a private, password-protected network, you'll see a padlock icon beside the network's name. If you don't know the password, you're not getting on. If it's an open network (open to the public), then you won't see the padlock icon, and you can just tap on the network, where you'll be connected to the Web, and you can start browsing.

---

iTip: A Free App for Finding Wi-Fi Hotspots

There's a great free app you can download from the App Store that helps you find nearby Wi-Fi hotspots. It's from JiWire, Inc., and it tracks over 200,000 Wi-Fi hotspots around the world. To download it, go to the App Store, tap on Search, enter "JiWire" and you'll find it in just a few seconds. They also have an app that only finds free Wi-Fi hotspots.

Using the Safari Web Browser

Once you've got a Wi-Fi connection, you use the Safari Web browser to visit websites. There's a field at the top of Safari where you enter the Web address (URL) of the site you want to visit, so tap once on that field and the keyboard appears at the bottom of the screen. Type in the Web address of the site you want to visit, then press the blue Go button in the bottom-right corner. Once the website appears, you can get a wider, larger view by turning your iPod touch sideways. If you tap twice on any part of the webpage, it zooms in and has that area fill your screen. To zoom back out, tap twice on the screen again. You use your finger to scroll up, down, or side-to-side on the page. To access a link you see on a webpage, just tap on it. To save the page as a bookmark, tap the + (plus sign) button on the menu bar at the bottom. To reload the page, tap the circular arrow button on the right side of the address field. To erase the existing address (so you can type in a new one), tap on the address field, then tap on the little gray X on the far-right side of it. To go to a previously viewed page, tap the Left Arrow button at the bottom of the screen.

---

iTip: Using the ".com" Button

At the bottom of the keyboard, to the left of the blue Go button, is a ".com" button, and one tap on it types in ".com" for you. If you press-and-hold on it, it brings up a pop-up menu with .net, .edu, and .org.

Using the Built-In Google Search

You don't have to go to Google.com to do a Web search, because it's built right into the Safari Web browser on your iPod touch. In Safari, just tap on the **Google search field** to the right of the address field, and the keyboard will appear. So, if you know the URL you want, use the address field. If you don't, tap on the Google search field and type in the search term you want. If you change your mind, tap the Cancel button at the top right.

---

iTip: Changing Search Engines

*If you don't want to use Google as your built-in search engine, you can choose Yahoo! instead by going to the Home screen, then tapping on **Settings**, and in the Settings screen, tapping on **Safari**. When the Safari settings screen appears, tap once on **Search Engine** and it brings up a screen where you can change your search provider by tapping on Yahoo!*

Working with Multiple Webpages

If you're on one webpage and you tap a link to visit another page, that page might be set up to open in a separate window (which is no problem—a new window will open to display that page). So now, you have multiple webpages open in Safari, and to see the various pages you have open, tap once on the little **Pages button** in the bottom-right corner. This shrinks the current page down to a smaller thumbnail size, and now you can scroll through the thumbnails of any open pages by swiping your finger left and right on the screen. To close one of these pages, just tap the red X in the upper-left corner of the thumbnail.

---

iTip: Accessing Bookmarks

*If you've saved any sites as bookmarks, you can access your Bookmarks list by tapping on the **Bookmarks** button (it looks like an open book) on the menu bar of your Safari screen. This brings up a list of your bookmarked sites and bookmark folders, and to visit one of those sites, just tap on it in the list (or tap on the folder, then on the bookmark).*

Importing Bookmarks from Your Computer

You can have the bookmarks on your computer automatically copied over to your Safari Web browser on your iPod touch, but you have to turn this feature on. First, connect your iPod touch to your computer for syncing, and then when its Preferences appear in iTunes, click on the Info tab in the main window, and scroll down until you see Web Browser. This is pretty easy because there's only one option here—**Sync (your Web browser) Bookmarks**. Turn on that checkbox and click Apply, and bookmarks from your computer's Safari Web browser (on a Mac) or from Microsoft Internet Explorer (on a PC) will be copied right into your Safari Web browser on your iPod touch.

---

iTip: Deleting a Bookmark

*To delete a bookmark, just tap on the Bookmarks icon, then tap the **Edit button** in the bottom-left corner. This adds little red minus signs before each bookmark, and if you tap on one of those, a red Delete button appears on the right side of that bookmark. Tap on the red Delete button to remove that bookmark. To delete a bookmark in a folder, tap on the folder first, then tap on the Edit button.*

Completing Online Forms

If you wind up buying something from a website, you're going to have to provide your name, address, payment info, etc., in an online form, and luckily Safari lets you do that in a surprisingly easy way. If it's just a text field you need to complete, then you simply tap on the field and the keyboard appears, so you can enter your info. Easy enough, but what do you do when you come across a pop-up menu (like one for the month and year your credit card expires or what state and country you live in)? When that happens, just tap on the pop-up menu and a special Safari window appears with the menu choices in a "flick wheel," where you can flick the wheel up or down with your finger until the choice you want appears, tap it to put a checkmark beside it, then tap the Done button.

---

iTip: A Shortcut for Not Syncing with iTunes

*If you want to charge your iPod touch, but you don't actually want it to sync with iTunes, you can temporarily stop syncing by pressing-and-holding the **Command and Option keys** (or the **Ctrl and Shift keys** on a Windows PC), while connecting your iPod to your computer, until you see the iPod appear in the Source list on the left.*

Watching YouTube Videos

If you have Wi-Fi Internet access, you can watch videos from the online video sharing site YouTube.com. From the Home screen, tap on **YouTube**, then tap on Search (at the bottom). Tap on the search field to get the keyboard, type in what you're looking for, and tap Search. The results appear in a list below the search field. To watch one of these videos, just tap on it, then turn your iPod touch sideways (videos always play in this wide mode). A set of controls will appear for pausing the video, jumping to the next video, replaying the video, and for adjusting the volume. To hide these controls, tap the screen. To bring them back, tap it again. To save a video as a favorite (so you can jump right to it next time), tap on the Favorites button at the left of the controls. Tap Done to get to a More Info screen or back to your search. At the bottom of the YouTube screens are buttons to take you to the featured videos of the day, YouTube's most viewed videos, your favorites, and if you tap the More button, you'll get menus that let you jump to the most recent videos, top rated videos, a History (list) of the videos you've watched, your videos, your YouTube subscriptions, and any YouTube playlists you've created.

---

iTip: Getting More Video Info

To see more information about a YouTube video, tap the little blue arrow button to the right of the video's name. This takes you to a screen with buttons to save this video as a favorite, save it to a playlist, or share it, and it gives you a list of related videos, as well. Tap the blue arrow button at the top, and you'll get a detailed description of the video.

Syncing Your Calendar

You can sync your calendar on your computer with your iPod touch, if you use either Apple's iCal or Microsoft Entourage on a Macintosh (to sync with Entourage, your calendar must be synced with Sync Services first), or if you use a Windows PC, you can sync your calendar from Microsoft Outlook. When you connect your iPod touch to your computer for syncing, it will upload your calendar information automatically once you've turned on the **Sync Calendars checkbox** on the iPod Preferences Info tab. *(Note:* If you have a MobileMe account, or a Microsoft Exchange account at work, you can also sync your calendar wirelessly via Wi-Fi.) To see your synced calendar info, start at the Home screen and tap the **Calendar icon**. You can view your calendar as one long scrolling list, or in a more traditional calendar view. To view by day, tap the Day button at the bottom of the screen, or tap the Month button to view the entire month (as shown above). In the Month view, if you see a small dot appearing below the date, that means you have an event scheduled for some time that day. To see the event, tap once directly on that day and that day's events will appear below the calendar. If you tap the Day view, it shows you the entire day by time, starting at 12:00 a.m. In Day view, you can navigate to other nearby dates by tapping the Left or Right Arrow buttons near the top of the screen. Anytime you want to jump to today's calendar, just tap the Today button in the bottom-left corner of the screen.

Syncing Your Contacts

If you're a Macintosh user, there are four applications that let you sync contacts directly from your computer to your iPod touch, and they are: (1) your Mac's Address Book application, (2) Microsoft Entourage (your Entourage Address Book must be synced with Sync Services first), (3) Yahoo! Address Book, or (4) Google Contacts. If your contacts are in any one of those four and your iPod is set to automatically sync, when you plug it into your computer, iTunes launches and syncs the contacts on your computer with your iPod touch. If not, go to your iPod Preferences Info tab and turn on the **Sync Address Book Contacts checkbox** (or choose to sync Yahoo! or Google contacts, instead). Pretty simple stuff.

If you're a Windows user, it works pretty much the same way, but the four contact managers it supports direct syncing from are: (1) Yahoo! Address Book, (2) Windows Contacts, (3) Microsoft Outlook, and (4) Google Contacts. Of course, if you have a Mobile Me account or a corporate Microsoft Exchange account, you can sync your contacts wirelessly.

Once your contacts are in your iPod touch, to see them, start at the Home screen and tap on **Contacts**. You can scroll through them using your finger on the touchscreen to flick the list upward or downward. To see a contact's info, just tap on the name. To create a new contact, tap the + (plus sign) button in the top-right corner of the screen. Tap on the various fields, and from the keyboard that appears, type in the contact information. When you sync with your computer again, any contacts you added in your iPod touch will be copied over to your computer. If your contact manager supports them, you can have contact groups on your iPod touch, as well.

Adding an Email Account

If you choose not to have your email accounts brought over from your computer through iTunes (this is done on the iPod Preferences Info tab), you can add them directly on the iPod touch. To do this, tap on **Mail** from the Home screen. This brings up the Welcome to Mail screen with links to Microsoft Exhange, MobileMe, Gmail, Yahoo! Mail, and AOL, where your iPod already knows all the geeky settings. If you're email isn't one of these, tap Other, where you'll need to know at least your username, password, and email address. You also may need to know your:

- email server type: POP, IMAP, or Exchange
- incoming server address (a.k.a. POP server): mail.domain.com
- outgoing server address (a.k.a. SMTP server): smtp.domain.com

Also, most outgoing mail servers require some kind of password for sending mail when you're not on their network. You'll need to check with your ISP to find out what settings to use. Most ISPs display this info in the Help section of their websites. When you set up your account, you probably received an email with all of this info.

If you need to add another account, tap the **Settings icon** on the Home screen, then tap on **Mail**, **Contacts**, **Calendars**, then under Accounts, tap **Add Account**.

Checking Your Email

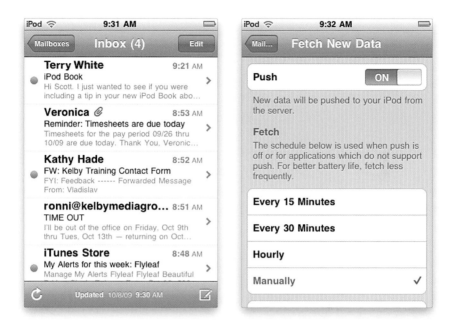

When you tap the **Mail icon** on your Home screen, as long as you have a Wi-Fi connection, it automatically checks for new email messages and puts them in your Inbox (if you've already been working in Mail, and want it to check for new incoming mail, just tap the circular arrow button in the lower-left corner of the screen). You can have Mail automatically check for new incoming mail on a schedule (like every 15 minutes, every 30 minutes, or every hour) using the Fetch feature, or you can check for new email manually (by pressing that circular button every time). Also, you can set up your Mail app to let you know each time an email arrives using the Push feature (the only downside to this is that it uses up your battery life faster). You set up both of these features (Fetch and Push) by going to the Home screen, then tapping on the **Settings icon**. In Settings, tap on **Mail**, **Contacts**, **Calendars**, then tap on **Fetch New Data**. To turn on Push, just tap the Off button. If you leave Push off (to save battery life), and you want to use the Fetch feature to automatically check at a time interval, just tap on the one you want in the Fetch portion of the screen.

---

iTip: Changing Your Mail Preferences

While you're in the Mail, Contacts, Calendars settings screen, you can set all sorts of options for how your iPod touch handles your email, including how many messages are displayed at one time, how many lines of your message you see as a preview, and things like showing the To/Cc label, etc. Just scroll down to see your options.

Reading Your Email

Once your email is set up and the messages start rolling in, they'll be listed under the account that you set up. Unread messages will have a blue dot to the left of them. By default, the iPod touch displays the first two lines of each message. You can then decide which emails you want to read in what order. When you want to display the entire email, just tap on the one you want to read and the email body will be displayed. You can scroll down the message by flicking your finger up on the screen. It's kind of counterintuitive at first because it's the opposite of the way you do it on your computer. Just think of flicking as the way you want the message to move. You want it to move up, so that you can read more of what's below. If the type is too small, you can use the pinch feature to zoom in and out: using two fingers on the display, such as your index finger and thumb, spread them out to zoom in on the message, then pinch them in to zoom back out. You can also pan around the message by simply moving your finger around on the display in the direction you want the message to move. You can use the Up and Down arrows in the upper-right corner to navigate to the next message or previous message.

---

iTip: How to Quote Part of an Email in Your Reply

You can quote a part of the original email in your reply by highlighting the text (see the copy-and-paste tip on page 104), then tapping the left-facing arrow at the bottom of the screen, and tapping Reply. Now that text will appear below your signature.

How to Email a Photo

You can sync photos to your iPod touch the same way you do on your iPod nano or classic (see Chapter 5 for more on importing and viewing your photos). So, if you have a photo on your iPod touch that you want to email to someone, from the Home screen, tap on **Photos**, then tap on the album your photo is in, and tap once on the thumbnail of the photo you want to email (if you need to see the photos full screen to pick the right one, just tap on a thumbnail, then swipe your finger across the screen in the direction you want to scroll. If your photo bounces like it's hitting a wall, you've reached the end of that album, so swipe back in the other direction). Once you see the photo you want to email at full-screen size, tap the icon in the bottom-left corner of the screen, and a list of things you can do with that photo will pop up. Tap on **Email Photo**, and it automatically takes you to a new email message screen with that photo already attached to the email. All you have to do is type in an email address, add any message you want, and tap Send.

---

iTip: Navigating a Photo Slide Show

Slide shows on the iPod touch work pretty much the same way as they do on the iPod nano or classic, including adding music (see Chapter 5 for more on this). On the iPod touch, though, you can stop your slide show by tapping the screen once. To return to the album thumbnail screen, once the slide show is stopped, tap the name of your album in the top-left corner of the screen. The slide show options (like the type of transition, how long each photo appears onscreen, etc.) are under Settings on the Home screen.

Make a Photo Your Startup Wallpaper

When you wake your iPod touch from sleep (and believe me, it will be asleep a lot), you're greeted with an unlock screen. By default, this unlock screen uses a NASA photo of the earth taken from space (which seems to be pretty much where all photos of earth are taken from these days). However, you can choose any one of your own photos for this background wallpaper instead. Start at the Home screen, tap on **Photos**, then tap on **Photo Library**, and find the one you want to use as your wallpaper. Tap on it to see it full screen. Now, tap once on the little icon in the bottom-left corner, and three buttons appear for your photo options (if you have a MobileMe account, you'll get a fourth button). Tap **Use As Wallpaper**, and you'll get a chance to move it around or scale it to fit better, then when you're satisfied, tap Set Wallpaper.

---

iTip: Pinch to Zoom

To get a closer look at any photo, just tap on the photo to see it full screen, then pinch two fingers together in the center of the screen and spread them outward to zoom in. To zoom in tighter, pinch outward once again. To return to the normal-size view, just double-tap on the screen.

Using Maps to Find Just About Anything

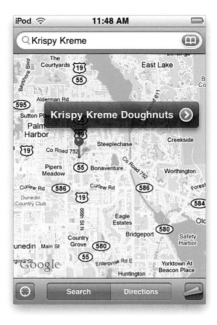

The built-in Maps app is pretty darn amazing—using a Wi-Fi connection, it lets you instantly find anything from the nearest golf course to a dry cleaner in the next city you're traveling to, and can not only give you precise directions for how to get there, it can give you the phone number, in case you need to call ahead. Here's how to use it: Start at the Home screen and tap on **Maps**. When the Maps screen appears, you'll see a search field at the top where you can enter an address you'd like to see on the map. However, before you type in your search, tap the circular **Locate Me button** in the lower-left corner, so that the iPod touch will know where you are. Then it will find the location of the business that you search for that's closest to you. For example, let's say you'd like to find the nearest Krispy Kreme donut shop (not that I'd actually ever search for one—wink, wink). You'd tap once on the search field to bring up the keyboard, then you'd type in the name of the business, and tap the Search button. In the example shown above, I entered "Krispy Kreme," and on the Google map of my area, a red pushpin appeared on the nearest location. A little pop-up appears with the name of the location that's closest, and if you tap the blue arrow in that pop-up, it takes you to an Info screen for that particular location. If you want to find a business that isn't near you, just add the city into the search. For example, typing "Krispy Kreme, Atlanta, Georgia" would locate the ones in, or close to, Atlanta, Georgia.

Finding Your Contacts on the Map

If you've included a street address for a contact, you're just a couple of taps away from seeing that address on the map. Just go to your All Contacts list (from the Home screen, tap on **Contacts**), tap on their name or do a search to find them, and when their **Info screen** appears, tap once on their address. This automatically takes you to the Maps app and pinpoints their address on the map. Better yet, once the map appears, tap on the curled page button in the lower-right corner of the screen, then tap on the Satellite button, and it shows you a satellite photo of their house or place of business. To zoom in for a closer look, just double-tap on their location on the screen. Each double-tap will zoom you in that much closer.

Getting Driving Directions

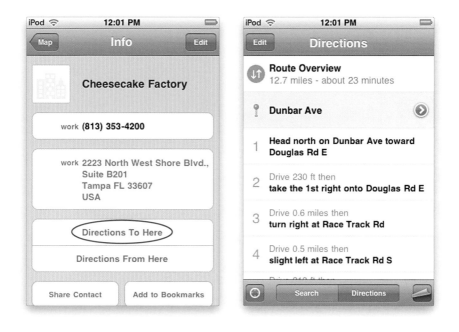

You can use the Maps app to get step-by-step driving directions to any location, and from any location. Here's how: Start at the Home screen and tap on **Maps**. Let's say you want directions to your favorite local restaurant—for me, it's Cheesecake Factory. Tap the Search button at the bottom of the Maps screen, then type in the name of the location you want to drive to, and tap the Search button again. Once it drops a pin on the map for the restaurant you want to drive to (if there's more than one pin, tap on the pin for the location you want), tap the little blue arrow button to the right of the pin's name. This will bring up the Info screen for the restaurant, including the phone number, so you can call and make reservations. Now tap the **Directions To Here button**, and this will take you to the Directions screen. Just tap the **Route button**, and the iPod touch automatically figures out where you are and plots your route accordingly. If you want turn-by-turn directions, just tap the little curled page button at the bottom right of the Overview screen showing your route, and tap List. This will give you turn-by-turn directions.

---

iTip: Switch Back to Map View

It you're having the Maps app give you directions from one location to another, with a street–by–street, turn–by–turn list of directions, if you tap on any of those directions, it instantly switches back to Map view to pinpoint exactly where that list item appears on the map between the two locations.

Drop a Pin on the Map

There will be times that you may not know the name of the business, or even the address, you're trying to get to. No problem! If you can find its general location on the map, you can use the Drop Pin feature to put a pin anywhere on the map you'd like. Once that pin is in place, you can then use it as a reference point to get directions from where you are to the location that's marked by the pin. Tap on **Maps** from the Home screen. Next, navigate the map to the general vicinity that you want to go to—you can do a search for a city, or a street, or anything else that's in the area. Then, tap the little curled page button in the lower-right corner of the screen to expose the additional Maps options. Tap on **Drop Pin** to put a pin on the map. You can then move the pin around by just tapping on it and dragging it with your finger. Once the pin is in place, tap the pin, then tap the blue arrow button, and tap Directions To Here. This brings up the Directions screen, where you can tap the Route button at the bottom, and the iPod touch will plot a route from your current location to the location of the pin.

Display More Information on the Map

The iPod touch not only has the ability to show your location and route, but it also can show a satellite view and even the current traffic conditions. To get to these options, just tap the **curled page button** in the lower-right corner of any of the Maps screens. Tapping Map shows you an illustrated map of the location that you search; Satellite will show you an actual satellite photo of the location you search; and Hybrid shows you the Satellite view with the street names—this is kind of the best of both worlds. Tapping List will show you turn-by-turn driving directions. The Show Traffic button adds real-time traffic flow info for the major highways (green for more than 50 mph, yellow for 25–50 mph, red for less than 25 mph, and gray if there's no data).

---

iTip: Locate Yourself on the Map

*The iPod touch uses Wi–Fi hotspots to figure out your current location. Tap the **Maps button** on the Home screen, then tap the **Locate Me button** at the bottom left of the screen to have it find your position on the map. Once it knows where you are, Maps can then be used to search the surrounding area for the nearest businesses and services that you want to find. Just type "pizza" in the search field, tap Search, and Maps will locate all the local pizza joints close to your location.*

Use Map Bookmarks

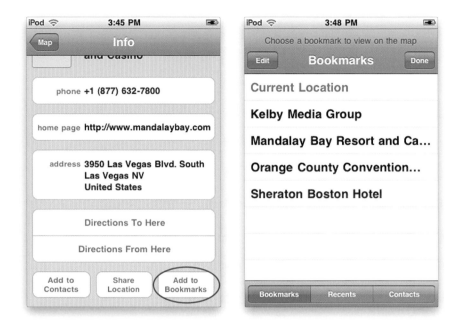

If you're traveling and you want to always be able to get back to the same place or have the same starting point (say your hotel) for each location you want to get a route to (or you get directions to places from home or work a lot), you can save your favorite locations as bookmarks. You can create a Maps bookmark from any of your search results or a dropped pin. Just tap the blue arrow button to the right of the pin's name that you wish to create a bookmark for, and then tap **Add to Bookmarks**. You'll be given the opportunity to name the bookmark whatever you like. Then tap the Save button. Now, the next time you want directions to or from that location, you can use your bookmark as a start or end destination in the Directions fields. Just tap Directions at the bottom of the screen, and then tap in either the Start or End field and you'll see a little **Bookmarks button** on the right (if the field already has a location in it, simply tap the little X at the right end of the field to clear it). Tap the Bookmarks button and tap Bookmarks at the bottom of the screen to bring up your list to choose from. Tap on the one you want, then tap the Route button, and you'll be on your way.

---

iTip: Recents Button Keeps Track

*The iPod touch will also keep track of your most recent Maps searches, so even if you didn't bookmark a location that you recently searched for, it may still be in your Recents (tap the **Recents button** at the bottom of the Bookmarks screen) and therefore accessible as a start or end point.*

Seeing Your Local Weather

Start at the Home screen and tap on **Weather**. The default city is Cupertino, California (where Apple's headquarters are located), but you can change it by tapping once on the little "i" icon in the bottom-right corner of the screen. You'll see a little red button with a – (minus sign) in front of the city. Tap on that button and a Delete button will appear to the right. Tap it and Cupertino is deleted. To add your own city's weather, tap on the + (plus sign) in the top-left corner and, using the keyboard that appears, type in your city and state or city and country, then tap the Search button. It will then display your city in a list (provided, of course, that it found your city), and all you have to do is tap on your city name, then tap the blue Done button in the upper-right corner, and you're just a tap away from your local weather. By the way, the color of the Weather screen lets you know whether it's day (blue) or night (purple) in the city you're looking at. To add more cities, click the + button again; just flick across the Weather screen to see your other cities. You can re-order the cities in the list view by tapping on the triple-line icon to the right of each one and dragging them up or down in the list.

---

iTip: Getting Even More Info in the Weather App

*On the bottom–left corner of each weather forecast screen is a little **Yahoo! logo**. Tap on that logo, and it takes you to a Yahoo! webpage with information about that city, including a city guide, today's calendar of events, photos, and more.*

Using the Calculator

When you tap the **Calculator icon** on your Home screen, it will bring up a basic calculator (as shown above, on the left). This calculator has all the basic functions that you'd expect (add, subtract, multiply, and divide), but it also has a built-in memory function. If you want a more sophisticated scientific calculator, just rotate your iPod touch on its side and you'll get the scientific calculator you see on the right instead. Pretty clever!

---

iTip: Clear Entry

*If you make a mistake while entering a series of numbers, you don't have to start over. Just tap the **C key**, which will perform a Clear Entry, and then you can simply re-enter the number.*

Getting Stock Quotes

You can monitor the current quotes for stocks in your portfolio directly from your iPod touch. Start at the Home screen, then tap the **Stocks icon**. When the Stocks screen appears, by default, it shows the Dow Jones Industrial Average and a few other stock indexes, along with a default list of stocks (Apple, Google, and Yahoo). You can delete any of these and add your own stocks to monitor by first tapping on the little "i" icon in the bottom-right corner of the screen. This brings up a list of the current indexes and stocks being monitored with a red circular – (minus sign) button before each listing. Tap on the red – button for the stock you want to remove and a Delete button appears to its right. Tap the Delete button and that stock is removed. To add a new stock (or index), tap the + (plus sign) button in the upper-left corner, which brings up the Add Stock screen. Type in the company name, index name, or stock symbol (if you know it) on the keyboard, then tap the blue Search button at the bottom-right corner of the screen. When it finds your company, it will display it in a list. Tap on the company name and it's added to your list of stocks. To add more stocks, tap the + button again. When you're done, tap the blue Done button in the upper-right corner. You can add as many stocks as you'd like, and to see other listings, just scroll down the screen by swiping (Apple calls it "flicking") your finger from the bottom of the screen up

Making Quick Notes

There's a Notes app for taking quick notes you want stored on your iPod touch. To get there, start at the Home screen, then tap the **Notes icon**. You'll see a list of any notes you've already taken. If you haven't created any notes yet, it figures you're there to create a new note, so it takes you to (no big surprise) the New Note screen. Type in your note (using the keyboard at the bottom of the screen), then tap the Done button in the upper-right corner when you're finished. This hides the keyboard and displays your note full-screen. To return to your list of notes, tap the Notes button in the top-left corner. To read any note in the list, just tap on it (each note automatically displays the date and time it was created at the top of the note). To delete a note, tap on it, then in the next screen, tap on the Trash button at the bottom of the screen.

---

iTip: Quickly Edit a Note

In the Notes app, to quickly edit an existing note, just tap on it in the Notes list. Then, when the note appears full screen, just tap anywhere on the note, and the keyboard appears—ready for editing. When you tap, if you tap on a word, your cursor appears right on that word. If you want to add to a note, tap just below your text.

Have Your iPod Sing You to Sleep

The iPod touch has a great sleep timer feature, which shuts down your iPod after a specific amount of time has passed. Here's how it works: Start at the Home screen, then tap on **Clock**, then tap on **Timer** in the bar at the bottom. In the Timer screen (shown above), choose how long you want your iPod to play before it puts itself to sleep by swiping your finger up and down to move the flick wheels. Once you've set the amount of time (let's say 25 minutes, for example), then tap on "When Timer Ends" and a list of choices appears. Tap once on **Sleep iPod**, then tap the blue Set button in the top-right corner of the screen. Now tap the large green Start button, and 25 minutes later your music will gently fade out and your iPod will put itself to sleep (just like a sleep timer on an alarm clock radio).

Using the Other Clock Features

In addition to the one on the previous page, there are three other clock features on the iPod touch (from the Home screen, tap on **Clock**). First, tap on **World Clock**, which lets you display the time in different time zones. To delete the default city, tap the Edit button in the top-left corner, then tap the red – (minus sign) button that appears before the city's name. This reveals a red Delete button to the right of the clock. Tap it once to delete that city/time zone. To add new cities, tap the + (plus sign) button in the top-right corner. This brings up the iPod touch's keyboard, where you can type in the city whose time zone you want to display. As you start typing the first few letters, it starts listing cities that start with those letters, so finding cities is quick and easy. When you find one you want (for example, London, England), tap on it, and the clock is created. If the face of the clock is white, it's daytime in that city. If it's black, it's night. Now tap the **Alarm button** at the bottom of the screen. To set an alarm, press the + (plus sign) button in the top-right corner, and a list of options appears, where you choose to repeat it one day a week, several days a week, or every day. You can choose the alarm sound (tap on Sound), whether you want a snooze option, and what you want to name your alarm. Below that, you choose the time in the same way you chose the sleep timer time on the previous page. If you tap Save, it adds an alarm to your list (you can create multiple alarms). Lastly, there's a Stopwatch feature that is incredibly simple—but more on that on the next page.

Using the Stopwatch

I love this Stopwatch feature because it's just so simple, efficient, and it has a really large readout. To get to it, start at the Home screen and tap on **Clock**. Then tap on **Stopwatch** at the bottom of the screen. There are only two buttons: Start and Reset. To start timing something, tap the green Start button. Once the stopwatch starts running, the green Start button is replaced by a red Stop button. To start over, tap Stop and then tap the Reset button. If you want to record lap times, just tap the Lap button (what used to be the Reset button before the stopwatch started running), and those times are listed in the fields below the two buttons. You can have lots of individual lap times (I stopped at 32 laps—man, was I tired), and you can scroll through the list of lap times just like you would scroll any list—by swiping your finger on the screen in the direction you want to scroll.

---

iTip: How to Quit an App That's Frozen Up

*If you're using an app and you think it's frozen, you can force the app to quit by pressing-and-holding the **Sleep/Wake button** on the top of your iPod touch for a few seconds until you see the red Slide to Power Off button appear. Once you see that button, Just press the **Home button** once and the app will Force Quit. Now just restart the app.*

Using Voice Control to Control Your iPod touch

To turn on Voice Control (available in the 32-GB and 64-GB models only), just press-and-hold the **Home button** until the **Voice Control screen** appears. You'll hear a beep, letting you know it's ready to accept your voice commands. To have it start playing music, say "play." To hear the next song, say (you guessed it) "next song," or to jump back, say "previous song." To hear the songs by a particular artist, say "artist," then the artist's name (so you'd say "artist, Lady GaGa," and your iPod will repeat the command, then start playing your Lady GaGa songs, provided, of course, that you have any). You can say "shuffle" to turn on the Shuffle feature, or say "What song is this?" to hear the title and artist of the currently playing song (cool, I know). To play a particular playlist, say "playlist" (pause a moment), and then the list's name. Here's one thing to keep in mind: Voice Control either works amazingly well and does exactly what you asked it for, or it gets your voice command wrong and totally plays something different than you asked for (just like the Voice Control in my car). When it gets something wrong, it generally just cracks me up, but depending on your disposition (or mood that day), you may not find it quite as funny.

Using the Built-in Voice Memos App

To record a voice memo, you need either the Apple Earphones with Remote and Mic (which have a microphone built into that thin little white bar attached to their cable) or a Bluetooth wireless headset with a mic. From the Home screen, tap on **Voice Memos**, then tap the red Record button (in the bottom-left corner) and begin talking. To pause your recording, press that same button again. When you're done, tap the Stop button in the bottom-right corner of the screen. Tap it again to get a list of your voice recordings (along with the time and date each was recorded, and how long each memo lasts). To hear a voice memo, tap on it in the list, then tap the tiny blue Play button that now appears to the left of it. To delete a memo, tap on it, then press the red Delete button at the bottom right. For more info on a memo, tap the blue arrow on the far right of the memo's name. To email a voice memo to someone else, tap on the one you want in the list, then tap the blue Share button at the bottom left. To record a new voice memo, tap the blue Done button in the top-right corner.

---

iTip: Trimming a Voice Memo Down to Size

*If your voice memo is too large to email, or you just want to keep a small part of it, first tap on the memo, then tap the blue arrow button to its right, and then tap **Trim Memo**. Now, just drag the yellow trim bar to the part of the memo you want, and tap Trim Voice Memo.*

Using a Wireless Bluetooth Headset

You don't have to use regular old-fashioned wired earphones any longer, because your iPod touch now lets you listen using a wireless Bluetooth headset instead. To turn this feature on, start by tapping on **Settings** (on the Home screen), then tap on **General**, and then on **Bluetooth**. Tap the Off button to turn Bluetooth on. Now you'll need to pair your iPod touch with your Bluetooth headset, so put your headset in discoverable mode, and soon you'll see it appear in the list of Bluetooth devices (but just seeing it there doesn't mean it's paired—it may ask you for a passkey or PIN, which would have come with your headset, so you'll have to look at the instructions for your Bluetooth headset to find that passkey, then enter that number into your iPod touch if, and when, it asks for it). Once it's paired, you're off and running wirelessly.

---

iTip: Using Bluetooth to Play Multiplayer Games

Want to play a two-player game wirelessly with a nearby friend who also has an iPod touch (and who has the same two-player game you do, of course)? This is called peer-to-peer gaming, and it uses your iPod touch's built-in Bluetooth wireless technology to pair with a nearby user's iPod touch (with their permission, of course), so you can play multiplayer games. You just need to both turn on Bluetooth, pair your iPod touches, then find a game (from the App Store) that supports two-player gaming.

Using the Nike + iPod Sport Kit for Runners

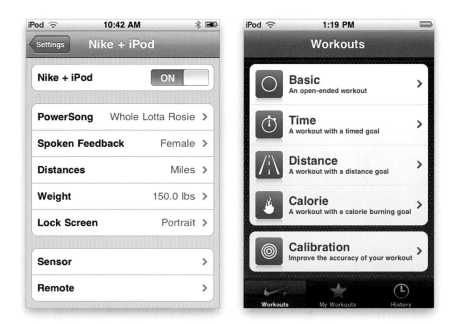

Runners are pretty psyched about the Nike + iPod Sport Kit for the iPod touch, because it's like having a personal trainer running with you (but one that keeps really copious stats and plays your favorite music while you're running). Your iPod touch already has the required receiver built in, but you need to get the special transmitter (available from either Nike or Apple for $29) that goes in your shoe. Once you install the transmitter (sensor) in your shoe, tap the **Settings icon** on your iPod touch's Home screen, scroll way down to **Nike + iPod**, tap on it, then tap the Off button at the top to turn it on. Next, tap **Sensor** to link it to your shoes. Now you can you track your progress, get motivation (both musical and voice), and set up custom workouts, timers for specific workouts (calorie goals or distance goals), and lots of other amazing stuff. You even have the option of uploading your results to your page on NikePlus.com to track your training progress over time.

---

iTip: Conserve Your Battery Between Runs

If you're not going to be using your Nike + iPod Sport Kit for a while, you should turn it off in your Settings to conserve the battery. You should also remove the sensor from your shoe to conserve its built-in battery.

Chapter Seven

Home
Sweet Home

iTunes Essentials

Now, I know what you're thinking: "How does Mötley Crüe's 'Home Sweet Home' tie into a chapter about the basic, most essential things you need to know about iTunes?" First, many of you will be using iTunes at home. (Unless of course, you're like my employees, who use iTunes all day long in lieu of working productively. In fact, when I'm roaming the halls, I'm not sure which I see more on their monitors—iTunes, eBay, Amazon .com, or CNN. Once I even saw someone with Photoshop open, but thankfully it was just because they were color-correcting an album cover they were going to use in iTunes. Whew—that was a close one!) Anyway, since some of you will be using iTunes at home, especially when you first get your iPod, I thought there was some loose thread I could use to connect your using your iPod there with the word "home" in "Home Sweet Home." Hey, it's fairly "loose" I know, but my backup plan was to use the song "Essential" by The Gravy, from their album "Lollipolyp." I didn't have a problem with the "polyp" part of it (as icky as that is), but if the chapter title was "Essential" and the subtitle was "iTunes Essentials," you'd think I took the easy way out, and you deserve more than that. You deserve a title that is so loosely related to the actual topic of the chapter that it takes more than 300 words to explain why I chose it. See, just when you think you've got me figured out, I ziq when you thought I'd zag (I have no idea what that means). Quick, turn the page before I think of something else to write here.

See Just the Info You Want

```
                    View Options

  ♫ Music

  Show Columns
    ☑ Album          ☐ Episode ID      ☐ Show
    ☐ Album Artist   ☑ Equalizer       ☐ Size
    ☐ Album Rating   ☑ Genre           ☐ Skip Count
    ☑ Artist         ☐ Grouping        ☐ Sort Album
    ☐ Beats Per Minute ☐ Kind          ☐ Sort Album Artist
    ☐ Bit Rate       ☑ Last Played     ☐ Sort Artist
    ☐ Category       ☐ Last Skipped    ☐ Sort Composer
    ☐ Comments       ☑ Play Count      ☐ Sort Name
    ☐ Composer       ☑ Rating          ☐ Sort Show
    ☐ Date Added     ☐ Release Date    ☑ Time
    ☐ Date Modified  ☐ Ringtone        ☐ Track Number
    ☐ Description    ☐ Sample Rate     ☐ Year
    ☐ Disc Number    ☐ Season

                          ( Cancel )  ( OK )
```

When you look at your Music Library in the iTunes main window, there are separate columns that display the song title, the artist, the album name, and so on. Some of it you probably will care about (like the song title, artist, time, etc.), and some of it (like the sample rate, beats per minute, or disc number) you might not care about seeing. Ever. Luckily, you can customize your columns and choose which ones are visible (and which ones are hidden). Press **Command-J (PC: Ctrl-J)** on your keyboard to bring up the iTunes **View Options dialog**. Select which columns you'd like to see by turning on the checkboxes next to the column names, and turn off the ones you don't care about, then click OK. Now only the columns you chose will appear in your main window.

---

iTip: Making Hidden Columns Visible

If at any time you decide you want a hidden column to be visible, just Right-click directly on one of the column headers. This brings up a contextual menu of column choices, so you can click on the one you want to see (hidden ones are the ones without a checkmark). To hide any column, you do the same thing, and it unchecks the column.

Finding a Particular Song

Once you have a couple hundred songs in your Music Library, finding one particular song can start to become time-consuming. When you have a few thousand, it's needle-in-a-haystack time, and that's why you'll want to use the **Search field** (in the upper-right corner of iTunes). Just begin typing the name of the song, album, or artist, and as you type, iTunes will immediately start displaying results (the more letters you type, the better it narrows things down) in the main window. To clear the search results and return to your full Music Library, just click on the little gray circle with an X in it (on the right side of the Search field). One more thing: if you click on the Music Library before you start your search, it searches through just your music (likewise, if you click on your Movies Library first, it only searches for movies). If you want to search within just a particular playlist, click on that playlist first, then start your search.

---

iTip: Searching Made Smarter

Let's say that you want to find the song "Black Cat" by Janet Jackson in your Music Library, so you type "black" in the Search field. This brings up 68 results when I try it, because it finds every song that contains the word "black"—everything from songs from Amy Winehouse's Back to Black album, to the Black Eyed Peas. But you can narrow your search right off the bat—click-and-hold on the little **magnifying glass icon** in the Search field, and choose Song from the pop-up menu. Now it only searches the names of songs, and not albums, artists, etc., which gets you to what you were searching for much faster.

Editing Your Song's Info

If you want to change, update, or add any information to a song, just Right-click on the song, and choose **Get Info** from the contextual menu. Click on the Info tab in the dialog that appears to see the fields where you can edit or add information about the song (when playing a song, this is where the info you see up in the status display at the top of iTunes comes from). Besides the basic info, you can also include other stuff, like the year it was recorded, your own personal comments, the song's composer, etc. When you're done, just click the OK button. If you want to edit a bunch of songs at once (like songs from a CD), just Command-click (PC: Ctrl-click) on all the songs you want to edit first, then Right-click on any of them, and choose Get Info. Now you'll get the Multiple Item Information dialog instead. Any info you enter here will be applied to all your selected songs.

---

iTip: Changing Just One Bit of Info (Like Album Name or Genre)

If you want to change just one bit of info on a song (like the artist or album name), you don't have to bring up the whole Get Info dialog—just click on the song first, then click once directly on whatever you want to change. This highlights that field, so you can type in a new name over the old one, then press the Return (PC: Enter) key to lock in your change.

Adding Song Lyrics

If you're really bad at remembering the words to songs, then "hang on—help is on its way" (sorry about that lame Little River Band reference). Here's the deal: you can embed lyrics into your songs (just like you embed the genre, the rating, album art, etc.) and these lyrics can be viewed right on your iPod nano, classic or touch. Here's how to set it up: In iTunes, first click on the song you want, then go under the File menu and choose **Get Info**. Click on the Lyrics tab, and type in the words (I usually find them on free lyrics websites—just do a Google search—then copy-and-paste them right into the lyrics field), then click OK. Once you've synced and the song is playing on your iPod, you can view the lyrics on your nano or classic by pressing the Center button a few times until they appear onscreen. On an ipod touch, tap on the album cover to see them. As luck would have it, there are two music file formats that you can't add lyrics to: QuickTime files and WAV files. So, what do you do? Convert them to a format that does support lyrics. Click on the file, go under the iTunes Advanced menu, and choose **Create AAC Version**. Bam. That's it—now you can add lyrics.

---

iTip: Skipping a Song

If you want to skip a song that's in a playlist, just turn off the checkbox that appears before the song's title. This also works when importing songs from an audio CD—it'll only import songs with a checkmark beside them, so if there's a song you don't want imported, just turn off its checkbox.

Use Browsing to Create Instant Playlists

Let's say you want to hear nothing but pop songs today, but you don't have a Pop playlist. Or maybe you just want to hear all your Dave Matthews songs but didn't make a Dave Matthews playlist either. Then you should try iTunes' Browse feature, which (with a couple of clicks) gives you a playlist of your favorite artist, genre, album, composer, or grouping. Here's how: Click on your Music Library on the left side of iTunes, then press **Command-B (PC: Ctrl-B)**, or go under the View menu and choose **Show Column Browser**. This gives you an Artist column to browse by on the left side of the main window. To browse by genre, go under the View menu, under **Column Browser**, and click on Artists to close that column, then go back and click on Genres to open that column. Click on Pop in the Genres column, and all your pop songs will instantly appear (well, at least all the songs that have been tagged with Pop as the genre). Just double-click the first song in the list, and it begins playing that list. It's that fast and easy. (*Note:* To turn off the Browse feature, press Command-B again. To view multiple Browse columns at the top of your main window, go under the View menu, under Column Browser, and choose On Top.)

---

iTip: How to Find the Song That's Playing Now

*While a song is playing in iTunes, of course you can go and do other things there (like sorting another playlist, editing song info, etc.). So, although you may be currently playing the song "Run this Town" by Jay-Z, you may not see that song highlighted if you're looking at or working on something else (maybe in an entirely different playlist). So, how do you find the song that's playing now? Just press **Command-L (PC: Ctrl-L)**, which instantly displays that song.*

Deleting Songs in a Playlist (Two Things You Need to Know)

If you want to delete a particular song out of a playlist, just click on it, and press the **Delete (PC: Backspace) key** on your keyboard. That's it—it's out of that particular playlist. Now, if you want that song completely out of iTunes altogether (and out of your life), first click on Music under Library on the left, then find the song, click on it, and press the Delete key. A dialog will pop up asking if you're sure that's what you want to do. If it is, click the **Remove button**. They're really concerned about you accidentally removing a song, so yet another dialog will appear asking, "Are you really, really sure?" (well, technically it asks if you want to keep it or move it to the Trash [PC: Recycle Bin]). Click **Move to Trash** and that puppy's gone! Also, the next time you sync your iPod, it will remove it from there, too. To delete multiple songs at once, just Command-click (PC: Ctrl-click) on all the songs you want to delete, then press the Delete key. If you want to select a whole group of contiguous songs, just click on the first song in the group you want to delete, then press-and-hold the Shift key, scroll down to the last song, and click on it. All the songs between where you clicked will be highlighted, and to delete them all with one keystroke, just press the Delete key.

Burning a CD of Songs

Burning a CD is a breeze, but there are a couple of things you should know: First, you can only burn playlists (not your entire Music Library), so click on the playlist you want to burn (by the way—if there's a song in this playlist you don't want on the CD, just turn off the checkbox in front of the song's name), then take a quick look down at the bottom center of the iTunes window to make sure you don't have more than 1.2 hours of music in your playlist (that's pretty much the amount of time you can fit onto an audio CD these days). If you have too many songs, delete some songs until you have less than 1.2 hours. Now click on the **Burn Disc button** in the bottom-right corner of iTunes, which brings up the Burn Settings dialog. Choose your settings, and click Burn. Now, the status window up top will ask you to: Please Insert a Blank Disc (that's your cue). Once you insert a blank CD, iTunes starts burning the songs. (*Note:* If you change your mind, click on the little X in the status window, which cancels the burn, but your formerly blank CD will no longer be usable.)

---

iTip: Clearing Your Play Count to Hide Your Tracks

iTunes keeps a running count of each time you play a particular song, but if at any time you'd like to wipe that play count clean (for example, if you're having friends over and you don't want them to see that you've played "The Loco-Motion" by Grand Funk Railroad 87 times), just Right-click on the song and, from the contextual menu, choose **Reset Play Count** *to reset your play count to zero. Your secret will now be safe forever.*

Setting the Gap Between Burned Songs

When you burn a playlist to a CD, iTunes adds a two-second pause between songs (which helps your CD player recognize individual tracks), but you can make that gap longer (or shorter), or you can eliminate the pause altogether (which you might want to do if you're listening to an audiobook or the recording of a speech). To do that, select the playlist you want to burn and click the **Burn Disc button** in the bottom right of iTunes. In the Burn Settings dialog, choose your desired length (in seconds) from the **Gap Between Songs** pop-up menu, and then click Burn.

---

iTip: Salvaging Damaged CDs

If your little sister has been using one of your prized CDs as a Frisbee, you're probably going to find that out when you play the songs in iTunes. It's going to have its share of scratches, junk, and other nasty stuff, which makes importing these tracks nearly out of the question—unless you know about this somewhat weird and obscure preference setting. To find it, go into the iTunes Preferences (found under the iTunes menu on a Mac or the Edit menu on a Windows PC), click on General at the top of the dialog, and then click on the **Import Settings button.** *Now turn on the checkbox for* **Use Error Correction When Reading Audio CDs.** *iTunes will then do its darnedest to correct a disc's trauma while importing, salvaging as much as it can. It doesn't work 100% of the time, but when it does, it's worth its weight in Starbucks coffee.*

Set Up Your CDs to Import Automatically

If you've decided to import your entire collection of CDs into iTunes, it's gonna take a while—especially since when you insert a CD, it doesn't automatically import the songs (instead, it figures you just want to listen to the CD, so it just shows you what's on the CD). However, you can set things up so when you insert a CD, iTunes automatically imports all the songs, then spits the CD out, ready for you to insert the next disc. Go to the iTunes Preferences (found under the iTunes menu on a Mac or the Edit menu on a Windows PC), at the top of the dialog, click on General, then from the When You Insert a CD pop-up menu, choose **Import CD and Eject**, and click OK.

---

iTip: Saving Hard Disk Space When Importing from CDs

When you import music from CDs, iTunes converts your songs into AAC format (which compresses the file size of your song files while maintaining CD-quality sound). But if you need even smaller files (and you don't mind a bit of a decrease in sound quality), you can import your CD songs as MP3s instead. Just go to iTunes' Preferences (under the iTunes menu on a Mac or the Edit menu on a Windows PC), click on General at the top, and then click the Import Settings button. From the Import Using pop-up menu, choose **MP3 Encoder***.*

Auto-Naming for Imported CD Songs

If you're importing songs from a CD, and you have a continuous Internet connection, iTunes automatically finds the names (and other background info) for all the songs you're importing. Here's what actually happens: When you import, iTunes will go to the Web and search within the massive Gracenote CDDB Internet Audio Database for the info on the CD you're importing. If it finds the information, iTunes will automatically download that information into each song, naming the songs (artists, album names, etc.) as it goes (pretty cool, eh?). If you don't have a continuous Internet connection, just add all of your songs to your iTunes Music Library or playlists, connect to the Internet, then under the Advanced menu, choose **Get CD Track Names**.

---

iTip: Adding Your Own Custom Genres

*Although iTunes comes with a preset list of popular genres, there are some it just doesn't include (like Salsa, Thrash, or New Wave), but you can add your own custom genres (like Death Metal or Opera). Just Right-click on any song, then from the pop-up menu, choose **Get Info**, and click on the Info tab. Now, just type the name you want for your "new" genre in the Genre field and click OK. If you want to create a genre that encompasses a number of different styles, just put a comma after each name (like Alternative, Punk, Soundtrack). Assigning multiple genres to a song will make that song appear in multiple categories when searching or browsing. For example, you might want the Etta James song "At Last" to have multiple genres, so it appears when you search for either Blues or R&B/Soul.*

Combining Two Tracks into One

Sometimes when you import a song from a CD, if the song has a lengthy introduction, it can get separated from the song. For example, look at Aerosmith's "Eat the Rich." It starts with a rap from Steven Tyler that actually has its own name ("Intro"), but if you hear this song on the radio, the two are played as one song—the intro goes right into the song. It really is one song, and when you import it from the CD, there's a decent chance iTunes will import it as one song, but if iTunes thinks these are two separate songs, there will be a gap of a few seconds between them. If that happens, no sweat—just Command-click (PC: Ctrl-click) on the two tracks before they're imported and then go under the Advanced menu and choose **Join CD Tracks**. Now, they'll import as one song, with no gap in between (you'll know that they're linked because a tiny bracket icon will appear next to the two tracks' names). By the way, if you ever want to really mess with rock history, you can select both tracks, go under the Advanced menu, and choose Unjoin CD Tracks. (*Note:* This whole joining thing can only happen *before* the CD tracks are imported into iTunes—not after.)

Playing Live Albums Without Pauses Between Songs

Multiple Item Information

Info Video Sorting **Options**

Volume Adjustment: ──────●──────
-100%   None   +100%

Equalizer Preset: None

Media Kind: Music

Part of a compilation: No

Remember position: No

Skip when shuffling: No

☑ Gapless album: ✓ No / Yes

Cancel   OK

On audio CDs there's always a little pause between each song, right? But if the CD is of a live performance (like The Fray Live), there aren't usually gaps (it's one continuous performance), so you probably want it to play on your iPod like it does on the CD—without the pauses between songs. (By the way, this doesn't just apply to live albums, it's also for classical albums, and some Pink Floyd albums, and Brian Wilson's classic "Smile," which should be one contiguous piece.) Anyway, this is called "gapless playback" (in iTunes speak) and here's how to turn it on: In iTunes, Command-click (PC: Ctrl-click) on all the songs you want to be gapless, then press **Command-I (PC: Ctrl-I)** to bring up the Multiple Item Information dialog. Click on the Options tab up top, turn on the **Gapless Album checkbox**, then choose **Yes** from the pop-up menu to its right, and click OK. That's it—the gaps are gone.

> **iTip: Changing Your Sort Order from First-to-Last to Last-to-First**
>
> *By default, iTunes columns are sorted in either alphabetical order (if you sort by artist, Aerosmith would appear up top and songs by the Zac Brown Band would appear near the bottom) or numerically (from the lowest number to the highest, though Ratings go from five-stars down to one-star. Go figure). Anyway, if you want the opposite (sorting from Z to A [which puts Zak up top], etc.), just click on the column, then click on the little upward-facing arrow to the right of the column's name (so if you're sorting by Artist, you'll see that arrow on the far right of the word "Artist"). This reverses things, so now you're sorting backwards.*

How Much Free Space Is Left on Your iPod

Want to know how much room you have left on your iPod? Connect your iPod to your computer, then click on it in the iTunes Devices list on the left side to see your iPod Preferences Summary tab in the main window. At the bottom of the tab is a **Capacity bar graph** that shows how much space is already taken by music, video, photos, or other stuff, and how much free space is left. That way, you know at a glance exactly what you have left.

---

iTip: A Few Status Window Shortcut Tips

That rectangular panel at the top center of iTunes (called the "status window") shows the name of the current song and the elapsed time, while the artist's name and the album name scroll continuously under the static song name. It also shows a progress bar, and how much time is left until the song is done. If you want to see how long a song is, click on the Remaining Time (on the right side of the progress bar). Want to see VU meters instead of all this stuff? Click on the tiny round button with the arrow on the left center of the status window. Click it again to return to normal.

Organizing the Songs on Your Hard Disk

If you have an MP3 song on your hard disk and you double-click on it, iTunes opens it and plays the song. It also creates an invisible shortcut (or alias) to that song from the folder on your hard disk. There's nothing wrong with this, but what you'll eventually have are folders scattered all over your hard disk with music in them. Well, you can make things much more organized than that (which makes backing up your music much easier) by having iTunes copy each song that it plays into the iTunes Media folder. That way, all of your music is in one place. To turn on this feature, go to the iTunes Preferences (on a Mac, it's under the iTunes menu; on a Windows PC, it's under the Edit menu), and at the top of the dialog, click on Advanced. In the Advanced options, turn on the checkbox for **Copy Files to iTunes Media Folder When Adding to Library**. Now you can click OK with the peace of mind that can only come from bringing order and harmony to your music world.

---

iTip: Consolidating Your Music

*If you've already got music scattered all over your hard disk, it's not too late—you can have iTunes go to all those folders and copy all the songs listed in your Music Library into the iTunes Media folder on your hard disk in just one click. Go under the File menu, under Library, and choose **Organize Library**. In the resulting dialog, turn on the **Consolidate Files** checkbox, and click OK. It wouldn't hurt if you played the song "Come Together" by The Beatles while you're doing this.*

Chapter Eight

Imaginary Player

Working with Playlists

Hey, it's not easy finding a song with the word "playlist" in it. Or a movie. Or a TV show. So, after doing some searching, I got as close as I was going to get with the song "Imaginary Player" by Jay-Z. Now, in the iTunes Store, there are two different versions of this song—one with the Explicit lyrics warning and one with the Clean label. Normally, I just go with the Clean version, because I'm a wholesome, family man myself. (However, one time I actually got "burned" when downloading the Clean version of a song. It was the song "1985" by Bowling for Soup. My wife heard the song on Radio Disney, told me about it, and when I found it in the iTunes Store, it had both Explicit and Clean versions, so of course I downloaded the Clean version for my son's playlist on my iPod. However, Apple's definition of Clean is obviously different than Radio Disney's. For example, in the Radio Disney version of the song, the second verse goes: "She was gonna be an actress. She was gonna be a star. She was gonna shake it, on the hood of Whitesnake's car." The "shake it" part's a little suggestive, but it's certainly not explicit. However, in the Clean version I downloaded, instead it says: "She was gonna shake her ass, on the hood of Whitesnake's car." Unsuspecting, I played it in front of my son, only once mind you, but of course he's memorized that line verbatim. Kids!) Anyway, this chapter isn't about the explicit version of either Jay-Z's or Bowling for Soup's song, but if it were, I'd probably sell a lot more books.

Putting Your Songs in Your Order

There are a number of different ways to have iTunes automatically sort the songs in one of your playlists (e.g., alphabetically by Name or Artist, by Genre, Rating, etc.), but what if you want to arrange the songs manually? You can do this by simply dragging the songs into the order you want, but this can only be done within playlists, not in your main Music Library. Also, to sort manually, you have to click in the very first column header from the left to make it the active column (it's called the Track Number column); otherwise, if another column (like Artist) is highlighted, the songs will already be auto-sorted, right? Right! So click in the far-left column, and begin sorting. One last thing: if you have the Shuffle option turned on (the second button from the left at the bottom left of the window), it won't let you manually sort. So if you're in a playlist, and you've got the first column highlighted, and you still can't sort, it's probably because Shuffle is turned on. Turn it off by clicking on the Shuffle button, and you're in business.

---

iTip: Finding Songs for Your Playlists Made Easy

Let's say you're creating a playlist of just classical songs. Rather than scrolling up and down through your entire Music Library searching for classical music, instead just click on the Genre column header, and it will re-sort your library by genre (press Command-J [PC: Ctrl-J] and turn on the Genre checkbox, if it's not one of your column headers). Now just scroll down until you see a bunch of songs with the Classical genre, then select them all and drag them over into your Classical playlist.

Deleting Songs (and Playlists)

Just click on a song (or Command-click [PC: Ctrl-Click] on multiple songs) in a playlist and then hit the **Delete key** on your keyboard (this only removes the song[s] from this playlist—it doesn't erase it from your Music Library). You delete playlists the same way: just click on the playlist you want to delete (in the list of playlists) and hit the Delete key (again, this just deletes the playlist—not the songs from your Music Library). Also, if you've got a song in one of your playlists that you don't want to delete, but you don't want to hear it right now, you can temporarily skip over it by turning off the checkbox that appears directly before the song's name (only checked songs will be played). To hear it again, just turn the checkbox back on.

---

iTip: Open a Playlist in a Separate Window

When you click on a playlist, it appears in the main iTunes window, replacing whatever was there before (like perhaps your Music Library). If you'd like a playlist to open in its own separate floating window (leaving your main window still open and untouched), instead of clicking on your playlist, just double-click on its icon or to the right of its name in the Source list.

Rearranging Your Column Order

If you're not happy with the default order of the columns (for example, if you'd prefer that the Album column was the fourth column, right after the Artist column), you can change them. Just click-and-hold on the Album column's header and drag it, until it appears right where you want it (you'll see a "ghost" image of your column as you move it, so it's pretty simple to move it where you want it). Moving columns, though, is specific to where you move them—if you move them in your Music Library, you'll only see the changes there, so when you click on a playlist, it'll show the default layout. But, now that you know how it's done, you can arrange the columns in any order you want (except for the Track Number column, which appears with playlists, and Name column—those are stuck there permanently).

---

iTip: Don't Like How iTunes Is Sorting Your Songs? Try This Trick

*You can give your songs a hidden name or artist name, just for sorting purposes (their real name will appear as always in iTunes, but now it'll be sorted the way you want). For example, if you sort your Music Library or playlist by Artist, and you have a song by 50 Cent, it won't wind up alphabetically under "F," instead it'll wind up at the bottom of your list. So, give it a hidden sorting name by clicking on the song, then pressing **Command-I (PC: Ctrl-I)**, and clicking on the Sorting tab. The left side of the dialog shows what you see in iTunes, but the right side is what iTunes actually uses when sorting. So, in the Sort Artist field, you'd type in "Fiddy Cent" and click OK. Now 50 Cent will appear sorted under "F."*

Combining Two Playlists into One

If you realize that you have two similar playlists (like one called R&B and one called Rhythm & Blues), you can combine them into one playlist by simply clicking-and-dragging one playlist onto another playlist, right within the Source list. Now, it's important to note that dragging the Rhythm & Blues playlist onto the R&B playlist creates a combined playlist (copying one playlist into another, which by the way, will cause any songs that were in both lists to appear twice, so you'll want to click the Skip button when iTunes asks you what you want to do with the duplicates). But, iTunes doesn't erase the Rhythm & Blues playlist. It's still there, if you want to delete it (just Right-click on it and choose Delete).

---

iTip: Printing Out Your Playlist

If you'd like a printed list of the contents of one (or more) of your playlists (hey, don't laugh—this is handy if your hard drive crashes and you haven't backed up in a while...or ever), just Right-click on the playlist that you want to print, and choose Export Song List. A Save dialog appears, so choose where you want to save the file on your hard disk, then click Save. iTunes exports your playlist as a tab-delimited text file, which you can open with a spreadsheet or database program, like Microsoft Excel, FileMaker Pro, etc., and then print it out.

How Rating Your Songs Helps

Even though you probably like all the songs you've imported into iTunes (or you wouldn't have imported them, right?), there are some songs in your Music Library that you like better than others. Well, if you give your songs a rating (using the one- to five-star rating system), iTunes will automatically add your top-rated songs into the My Top Rated smart playlist (which appears near the top of the Playlists list in the Source list). That way, anytime you want to hear just your favorite songs, there's already a playlist for them, and it updates live as you rate new songs (that's the beauty of smart playlists. For more on them, see the next couple of pages and check out the bonus chapter on the book's companion website at **www.kelbytraining.com/books/ipod6**). To rate a song, turn on the Rating column in your iTunes window (press **Command-J [PC: Ctrl-J]** and turn on the Rating checkbox), then just click directly on the song, and you'll see five little gray dots in the Rating column. Click-and-drag your cursor over these dots (from left to right), and as you do, a star appears over each dot (so to make it a five-star song, you'd drag over all five dots). To remove a star, drag back over it to the left (it's easier than it sounds). *Note:* On a Mac, you can rate the song that's currently playing in iTunes from the Dock by clicking-and-holding on the iTunes Dock icon and choosing your rating from the Rating submenu; on a PC, click on the down-facing triangle at the bottom right of the iTunes toolbar in the Taskbar, go under My Rating, and click on the stars.

Have iTunes Make Smart Playlists for You

```
                            Smart Playlist

☑ Match the following rule:

    Artist            ⬍     contains          ⬍                          ⊖ ⊕ ⋯

☐ Limit to  25    items    ⬍  selected by  random                  ⬍
☐ Match only checked items
☑ Live updating

?                                                        ( Cancel )  ( OK )
```

You can have iTunes make playlists for you, automatically, based on whatever criteria you'd like. For example, you could have it make a playlist of just songs you haven't heard in three months, or an instant playlist of songs that are 120 beats per minute or faster, or a playlist of nothing but songs you've rated as one-star (so you can hear them and decide if you even want these songs just taking up space on your computer). These automated playlists are called "smart playlists" and you create them by choosing **New Smart Playlist** from the File menu (or by pressing-and-holding the **Option [PC: Alt] key** and clicking the **Create a Playlist button** at the bottom left of iTunes). This brings up the Smart Playlist dialog you see above, where you get to choose from loads of different criteria options. When you create a smart playlist, it's added to the top of the list under Playlists in the Source list, and you can tell by the icon that it's a smart playlist (it's purple and has a little gear icon). Anytime you want to change the criteria for a smart playlist, just Right-click on it and choose Edit Smart Playlist. To add another line of criteria to your smart playlist, click the + (plus sign) button to the right of the last line of criteria (to take a line away, click the – [minus sign] button). If you want to add a subcategory to your criteria, then click the little … (ellipsis) button, and a subcategory appears below that line, which is tied to criteria above it. Also, I always keep the Live Updating checkbox turned on, so that if I add a new song, or change the rating of a song, etc., those changes are automatically reflected in the playlist (as if somebody is monitoring and updating your playlist for you. Sweet!).

A Smart Playlist Idea for Short Trips

Just to give you an idea of the simple power of smart playlists, here's a really easy smart playlist idea: If you only live 10 minutes from your job (lucky you), you probably don't want to listen to one long song all the way to work, right? So why not create a smart playlist of just short songs? Here's how: **Option-click (PC: Alt-click)** on the **Create a Playlist button** to create a smart playlist. When the dialog appears, from the first pop-up menu, choose Time; from the second pop-up menu, choose Is Less Than; and in the text field, enter "3:00." Now, when you play this smart playlist on your iPod on the way to work, you'll hear around three full songs, and you'll be at least one-third of the way through the fourth. Want another smart playlist idea? How about this one: Want to hear the same songs you heard exactly one week ago? Well, when you create your smart playlist, in the first pop-up menu, choose Last Played; in the second menu, choose Is; and in the text field, enter the date exactly one week ago today. By the way, you might as well name this smart playlist "Déjà Vu."

> **iTip: I Put of Bunch of Smart Playlist Ideas Together for You!**
>
> *I put some other really simple smart playlist ideas online for you to check out (it's a PDF in the same format, look, and feel as what you see here). You can find it on the book's companion website at* **www.kelbytraining.com/books/ipod6** *(see, I care!).*

Cutting Clutter with Playlist Folders

It's fairly easy to get sucked into "playlist mania" and before you know it, you have 600 playlists—one for every mood, every occasion, every genre, every band, every possible road trip, every…well, you get the idea. Anyway, if you need to bring some sanity to your playlist collection, you can create a playlist folder to organize all your playlists that share a common theme (with subfolders inside). For example, you could have a folder named "Parties" and inside that you could store all the playlists you use at parties (your Rave mix, Burning Man mix, Impromptu Vegas Hotel Room Party mix, Limo Party mix, etc.). That way, they're all tucked away in just one folder. If you want to see them all individually again, just expand the folder (as shown above). To create a playlist folder, just go under the File menu and choose **New Playlist Folder**. The new folder will appear under Playlists in the Source list (highlighted and ready for you to name), so you can easily drag-and-drop related playlists right into this folder. Once you've put multiple playlists into one folder, you can then "play the folder" and it will just play the playlists in that folder.

---

iTip: Another Way to Create Playlists

*You can also create playlists by first selecting the songs in your Music Library you want in a playlist (Command-click on them on a Mac; Ctrl-click on a PC), then going under the File menu and choosing **New Playlist from Selection**. Those songs will now appear in a new playlist in the Source list (it'll be highlighted, ready for you to name).*

Create a Genius Playlist in iTunes

The Genius feature automatically builds playlists for you based on the type of music you already listen to. For example, let's say you like the song "21 Guns" from Green Day. To have iTunes create a Genius playlist of other songs from your Music Library that are kind of that same style, first click on "21 Guns," then click the **Genius button** in the bottom-right corner of iTunes (shown circled here in red. If this is your first time using Genius, you'll need to click on Genius in the Source list and then click on Turn on Genius and log into your iTunes account). That's it—it looks through your Music Library, analyzes what you have, and puts together a mix based on you liking "21 Guns." What's scary about all this is it does a pretty darn good job (so much so, that a lot of people are absolutely hooked on Genius playlists now, because it's just fun seeing what it comes up with). If you don't like the first set of results, just click the **Refresh button** near the top-right corner (you'll also find controls there for choosing how many songs you want to include in your Genius playlist, and if you like a particular playlist it came up with, just click the **Save Playlist button**, and it'll convert it into a playlist for you).

---

iTip: Making a Smart Playlist Regular

Have you fallen in love with the current content of one of your smart playlists? Then have iTunes make a regular playlist from your smart playlist (that way, it doesn't auto-update anymore). Here's how: just click-and-drag your smart playlist up to the word "PLAYLISTS" in the Source list and when you release your mouse button, a new regular playlist will be created in the Source list with the contents of your smart playlist.

Let Genius Find Songs You Don't Own (Yet)

The iTunes Store has its own version of Genius playlists, but instead of choosing similar songs from your existing Music Library, it uses a research database of actual iTunes users to determine other songs you don't own that you'd probably like (in other words, if you like this one, you'll probably like...this one!). This feature is off by default, so to turn it on, click the **Show/Hide Genius Sidebar button** (the little left-facing arrow) in the very bottom-right corner. This adds a column to the far-right side of iTunes (seen above). At the top are other songs and albums from that same artist you clicked on that are available in the iTunes Store, then below that are Genius recommendations from the iTunes Store based on your current song. What I like about this is you can hear a 30-second preview of any song in this sidebar (by clicking on the little round **Play button** that appears before the song's name), and you can even buy the song and download it—all without actually going to the Store itself. Plus, like the regular Genius feature, it does an amazingly good job of finding songs you don't already own that you probably would like (I've found loads of great songs I either didn't know about, or had forgotten about, which is why those little 30-second previews are so valuable). Also, if you don't like their Genius recommendations, just click the **Genius button** (the one with the little atom in the bottom-right corner), and it'll generate a new list you might like better. To hide this Genius sidebar, just click the Show/Hide Genius Sidebar button again.

Genius Mixes Do All the Work for You

Metal Mix 2
Based on: Doro, Skid Row, Cinderella, & others.

On the previous pages, you learned about Genius playlists (where you click on a song, and then the Genius feature puts together a playlist of similar songs), but there's something you might like better, partially because it doesn't require any input from you whatsoever. This feature scans your Music Library and builds a bunch of different Genius mixes based on what it finds, putting similar songs together in their own mixes (it's kind of building little radio stations based on your own musical tastes). All you have to do is turn Genius on by clicking on Genius in the Source list, then clicking on the Turn on Genius button and logging into your iTunes account. If Genius is already on, go under the Store menu and choose **Update Genius**. Now, Genius Mixes will appear under Genius in the Source list. Click on it, and it displays sets of album covers that give you a sample of what's inside each mix. To see what the name of the mix is (and the names of some of the artists it's based on), move your cursor over the cover art and that information appears right below it. When your cursor is over the cover art, a little **Play button** appears in the center. To hear that mix, just click on it. To skip to the next song in the mix, press the **Right Arrow key** on your keyboard (to jump back, press the **Left Arrow key**). This is another one of those things you just have to try for yourself. My guess is you'll love it.

Using iTunes as Your Party DJ

This tip is way better than it sounds at first. There's a feature called the iTunes DJ, which automatically creates a party music playlist (based on some criteria you get to choose). But then it adds songs to this playlist automatically all night long, so the music at your party doesn't stop. That's fairly cool by itself, but on the next page I'm going to show you something that can make your iTunes DJ the talk of the entire party. First, let's get the iTunes DJ set up: Click once on **iTunes DJ** (it's the first thing listed under Playlists in the Source list) and it picks 15 songs from your Music Library to start your party. If you don't like the songs it chose, click the **Refresh button** in the bottom-right corner and it'll pick 15 other songs. If you want it to pull songs from a particular playlist (like a playlist you put together earlier of great party songs), you can choose that playlist from the **Source pop-up menu** at the bottom left of the main window. To the immediate left of the Refresh button is the **Settings button**. Click on that to choose things like how many of the already played songs still appear in the list, and to change the number of upcoming songs from the default 15-song queue to more (or less). If you want to make sure just your best songs in that playlist get played the most, turn on the Play Higher Rated Songs More Often checkbox. Now just double-click on the first song in the list, and your iTunes DJ will make sure the party music doesn't stop. Turn the page to take things up a big notch.

Letting Your Party Guests Control the Music

Here's where the iTunes DJ gets really cool: if any of your party guests have an iPod touch or an iPhone, they can use Apple's free Remote app to request songs, and even add songs to the iTunes DJ mix, without interrupting you from serving martinis. To turn on this feature, after you click on **iTunes DJ** in the Source list, click on the **Settings button** (at the bottom right), and turn on the **Allow Guests to Request Songs with Remote for iPhone or iPod touch checkbox**. You can also include a welcome message or instructions on how to request/add songs (just include whatever you want in the Welcome Message field), and you can choose whether guests can request songs from your entire Music Library or just a specific playlist (so, for example, if you're having a disco-themed party, you can make sure they only choose songs from your Disco playlist). Guests can also vote on which song already in the queue will play next, and you can add a password, so the neighbor next door doesn't start requesting Bay City Rollers songs (not that there would actually be any on your iPod, right?). Once this is set up the way you want it, when guests go to their iPhone/iPod touch and choose to request a song from their Remote app, they'll get to choose one from your playlist (or Music Library if you choose), and then that song becomes the next song to play. This is just one of those things that you have to have your party guests try, and they'll be talking about it for days (oh yeah, and that tasty rumaki).

Chapter Nine

Proof of Purchase
Using the iTunes Store

Apple changed the music industry forever when it introduced the iTunes Store with its "fair play" technology, which preserves the rights of the artists who make their music available for legal download. It was revolutionary, and more importantly, it worked. Now more than 11 million songs are available for legal download from the iTunes Store. I sometimes call it the ITS for short, because writing out "iTunes Store" each time gets really old really fast. Not just for me, mind you, but for you—the reader. That's why acronyms exist. People get tired of reading, writing, and even saying long names. For example, my full legal name (as it appears on my birth certificate) is: Stephen Charles Oscar Theodore Thaddeus Kevin Edward Lawrence Bradley Young. After painstakingly writing it out that way for more than 26 years, I finally came up with the acronym SCOTT KELBY instead, which is much easier to write, and best of all, its meaning is pretty obvious to your average person (kind of like IBM or UPS). For the next three years, I always wrote the acronym in all caps, but once I realized that most people knew what it stood for (like ASAP or NFL), I then dropped the cap on everything but the first letter of each word, making it just Scott Kelby. Now, about the name of this chapter—it's actually a band's name, Proof of Purchase, and (as of the writing of this book) you can find two of their songs on the ITS. I listened to the 30-second preview of their song "Fallacy," and it scared the livin' crap out of me. Don't ever listen to that preview with the light outs. It's way too Eerie, Creepy, and Scary. It's ECS.

Getting Around the iTunes Store

There's a link to the **iTunes Store** under Store in the Source list on the left side of iTunes (shown circled above). The iTunes Store is a lot like a website—there's a homepage and you click links to visit other pages in the Store (in fact, you can't access it without an Internet connection, so iTunes is like a Web browser for the Store). To get back to the homepage, click on the Home button that appears near the top-left corner of the iTunes main window. To navigate back to the previous page, press the Back button (to the left of the Home button). There are direct links to the stuff you're most likely to look for across the top of the main window. If you click on one of those links, it takes you to the main page for that topic. So if you click on Movies, you get the main Movies page, but you can jump directly to any category within Movies (like Comedy or Thriller) by moving your cursor over the link, and clicking on the little arrow that appears on the right to get a pop-up menu of categories. On the homepage, the top sellers in some of the categories (Songs, Albums, Movies, TV Shows) appear along the right side (to see more top sellers in those categories, click the See All button to the right of each one).

---

iTip: Navigation Keyboard Shortcuts

*Just like a Web browser, you can return to your previous page by using keyboard short-cuts. For example, to jump back one page, press **Command-[(PC: Ctrl-[)**—that's the Left Bracket key and it's immediately to the right of the letter P on your keyboard. To jump forward one page, press **Command-] (PC: Ctrl-])**—that's the Right Bracket key.*

Finding Stuff in the iTunes Store

The **Search Store field** (in the top right of iTunes) works for searching through the iTunes Store, but it works differently than searching through your own Library. That's because, when you're searching on your computer, it only searches one place: your Music Library, or Movies Library, or whatever you click on before you start your search. But a search in the iTunes Store searches everything the Store carries—from music, to movies, to TV shows, to podcasts, to audiobooks, etc. So, when you type in a word (like "Cars"), you're going to get a lot of results back that you can quickly narrow down by clicking on one of the categories in the Filter By Media Type section (Music, Movies, etc.) in the top left of the main window (shown circled here in red). So, for example, click on Movies, and now all you'll see in your search results are movies that have "Cars" somewhere in them (it could be as obvious as it being the title of a movie—like Disney's *Cars*. Or it could be the name, or part of a name, of an actor/actress/producer/director of a movie—like actor Terrence Carson, who was in the World War II submarine movie *U-571*, which shows up as a result for movies with the word "Cars").

---

iTip: Make Your Store Full Screen

*There's an option (which I love) that makes the iTunes Store fill the entire window (so it hides the Source list on the left side of the window, which is great because you don't use that list when you're shopping anyway). Just go under iTunes' Preferences, click on Store, then turn on the **Use Full Window for iTunes Store checkbox**, and click OK.*

You Can Browse in the iTunes Store, Too!

A good example of browsing in the iTunes Store is genre browsing, which really works well, because Apple assigned a genre (or category) to everthing in the Store. For example, to browse through all the Children's Music, just click on the **Browse link**, under Quick Links at the top right of the iTunes Store homepage, and then in the iTunes Store column on the left, click on Music, then click on Children's Music in the Genre column, and in the Subgenre column, click on All. The artists who have downloadable tracks will appear in the Artist column (the fourth column from the left), and if you click on an artist, all of their albums appear in the Album column at the top right. Click on an album and those tracks will appear in the main window. *Warning:* If you try this a few times in the iTunes Store, you'll most likely love it, and then you'll start using genre browsing in your own media Library, even though you thought you didn't like browsing. Hey, I'm just sayin'.

---

iTip: Almost Everything Is Clickable

There's more to the iTunes Store than meets the eye, because almost everything you see is a clickable link. So if you do a search and some album covers appear at the top of the window, try moving your cursor over the text beside an album—like over the artist's name. It's a link that'll take you to the album and all that artist's work. You can even click on the Explicit warning and you'll get a description of what "explicit" means. If you were wondering, it means "really naughty stuff."

A Source for Musical Inspiration

If you need a little musical inspiration, go to the iTunes Store, click the Music link at the top, then on the right side of the main window, scroll down to the More in Music section, and click on **See All** to the right of **Celebrity Playlists**. Apple has asked celebrities to create and publish their own iTunes playlists, and often their suggestions for songs are really good. You can sort by date added (to get the most recent playlists) or alphabetically by name using the pop-up menu in the top-right corner. Once you find a musician or celebrity that interests you, just click on that person's photo to see their picks and, most importantly, a note on why they picked 'em. Best of all, because these picks are sold in the iTunes Store, you can hear a 30-second preview of each suggestion. This may sound a little corny, but give it a try—I think you'll be surprised at some of the cool music your favorite celebrities and bands are listening to.

---

iTip: Make Your Own iMix

*With an iMix, you can publish your own playlist in the iTunes Store and share it with the world (so other people can see and buy your favorite songs). To create and publish your own iMix, just put together a playlist of your favorite songs within iTunes, then go under the Store menu and choose **Create an iMix**. iTunes will connect to the iTunes Store and your iMix will be live. To see other people's iMixes (and rate them), go to the iTunes Store homepage, click on Music, and on the Music page, click on **iMix** on the bottom right under More to Explore.*

Can't Find It? Try a Power Search

If the regular Search Store feature doesn't come up with what you were searching for, you can try a Power Search, which lets you really refine your criteria. To do a **Power Search**, go to the iTunes Store homepage and click on Power Search under Quick Links at the top right of the main window. Then, choose the type of media (movies, music, etc.) from the pop-up menu on the top left, and a more detailed search area will appear across the top of your main window (the Music Power Search is shown above). Now you can search in multiple areas (like searching by Artist, Composer, Song, Album, and/or Genre) all at once. Hey, it's worth a try.

---

iTip: Apple's Music Request Form

If you've searched the iTunes Store and the song you want just isn't available yet, what can you do? Tell Apple. That's right, Apple has a music request form, so you can tell them which songs you'd like to see added to the iTunes Store. To find this online form, visit www
.apple.com/feedback/itunes.html and when you get there, in the Comments field, tell them the name of the song(s) and the artist(s) you'd like to see added. It's no guarantee, but if you want it badly enough to let Apple know, you might not be alone, and the more times they hear it, the better chance you'll soon find it in the ITS. Give it a shot.

The Shortcut from iTunes to the iTunes Store

When you click on a song in your own iTunes Music Library, you'll often see a little arrow appear to the right of the song name, artist's name, and album name. Even though you're not in the iTunes Store, those are actually links to the Store—shortcuts to take you directly to that song's album in the iTunes Store (if you click the arrow to the right of the song or album name), or to a page where you'll find all of the artist's albums available in the iTunes Store (if you click the arrow to the right of the artist's name). Some artists even have a "feature page" that will appear when you click on the little arrow to the right of their name. You'll not only get a big fancy photo of the artist(s), but if you look around on this page, you're also likely to find a Biography link, and sometimes a link to the artist's website or iTunes exclusives, among many other links.

---

iTip: iTunes in Other Countries

*Want to take a peek at what the iTunes Store for Germany is like? Easy enough. Just start at the iTunes Store homepage, scroll all the way down to the bottom, and on the bottom right of the page, you will see a **flag icon**. Click on it and icons will appear representing each of the iTunes Stores in the world. To see what another country's Store is like (and see their top songs), just click on that country's icon.*

Buying Songs or Adding Them to Your Wish List

When you look at a song in the iTunes Store, you'll see a gray button to the right of the title with the price and the word **"Buy."** Click it, and it'll ask you for your password (to make sure it's really you), and then it begins downloading immediately (the songs download amazingly fast). If you want to buy the entire album, click the **Buy Album button** found beneath or to the right the album art. If you're not sure you want to buy a particular song (or album), you might just want to add it to your Wish List (so you can buy it later). Just click directly on the little down-facing arrow to the right of the Buy button, and from the pop-up menu, choose **Add to Wish List**. By the way, the Wish List feature is a great way to control your spending—just add the items you want to your Wish List, and you'll be able to see how much you're spending before you buy anything. To see the items in your Wish List (they can be movies, TV shows, etc.), go back to the homepage and click on **My Wish List** in the Quick Links section at the top right (you'll see a little tiny number beside the link showing how many items you currently have in your Wish List). Once you're there, you can buy any single item or all of 'em.

Upgrading Your Old Songs to Be DRM-Free

Originally, all songs in the iTunes Store had Digital Rights Management (DRM) protection, which allowed your songs to be played on a limited number of computers (only five). Now, the standard for songs in the iTunes Store is DRM-free (iTunes Plus), with no restrictions on songs for your personal use (or which MP3 players you can play them on). However, if you bought songs back before May 2007, you probably still have some DRM-protected songs in your Music Library, but iTunes can help. While you're on the homepage of the iTunes Store, click on **iTunes Plus** in the Quick Links section at the top right (you'll see a little number to the right of the link telling you how many DRM-protected songs you have), and all the DRM-protected songs in your Music Library will appear, where you can upgrade them (for 30¢ each at the time of this writing) to the DRM-free format (another benefit is this also replaces your old song with one that has the highest audio quality available from Apple). You can upgrade them individually or you can upgrade all of them at once by clicking the Buy All button (the full price and total number of songs are displayed to the right of the Buy All button).

---

iTip: How to Know If You Already Own That Song

To keep you from buying the same song twice, songs that you've already bought from the iTunes Store are not only grayed out, but if you look where the Buy button would normally be, it says "Purchased."

Allowing Multiple Simultaneous Downloads

When you buy songs or videos from the iTunes Store, they download in the order you purchased them. However, if you're on a serious buying spree, there's an option you'll want to know about that lets you download multiple purchases simultaneously, instead of one-by-one in order. To get to this option, you have to be downloading a song, because the checkbox that turns this option on is actually found in the Downloads window itself. Once a song is downloading, click on Downloads under Store in the Source list on the left side of iTunes, and you'll see the **Allow Simultaneous Downloads checkbox** (circled here) near the bottom of that window. Turn on this checkbox and it can download up to three items simultaneously, and if you've got more than that lined up to download, you can drag the queued-up downloads into the order you want them downloaded.

---

iTip: Pausing Downloads and Restarting Again Later

*If you're downloading a bunch of songs (maybe a whole album), a movie, etc., you can pause your download and start again later, when it's more convenient. To pause a download in progress, just click the little **Pause button** that appears to the right of the status bar and it will say "stopped" beside the download. To resume that download, click the circular arrow button that now appears to the right of the status bar. To pause all your downloads, click the **Pause All button** in the bottom-right corner of the main window. To resume them all at once, click the **Resume All button**. Once all your music (and/or videos) is downloaded and you click on a Library, this Downloads link will disappear.*

Why You Need to Back Up What You Buy

```
                        iTunes Backup

            Welcome to iTunes Backup

            Back up your iTunes library to CDs or DVDs.

              ● Back up entire iTunes library and playlists
              ○ Back up only iTunes Store purchases
              ☐ Only back up items added or changed since last backup

            To restore from a backup disc, open iTunes and insert the disc.

            Disc Burner:      MATSHITA DVD-R  UJ-85J

            Preferred Speed:  [ Maximum Possible ▲▼ ]


                                    ( Cancel )   ( Next )
```

In the back of your mind you're probably thinking, "Hey, if my hard drive ever totally dies, I'm covered, because Apple keeps a history of all my iTunes purchases, and if that mega-crash day ever comes, they'll let me download everything again, right?" Nope. Apple doesn't let you download anything again without paying for it again, so if your hard drive dies, so do all your songs, videos, etc. (purchased and otherwise). That's why it's *so* important to back up your purchases. To do this, go under the iTunes File menu, under Library, and choose **Back Up to Disc**. Then you get to choose whether to back up your entire iTunes Library or just the stuff you purchased from the iTunes Store (to a CD or DVD). You also can choose just to back up new stuff since the last time you backed up. Make your choice, then when iTunes tells you to, insert a blank disc and it'll take it from there. Keep poppin' in new blank discs until everything is backed up. Remember, if you don't back up, one day you're almost certain to lose your entire iTunes Store investment. So, back it up now (you'll thank me someday).

---

iTip: Seeing the Album Cover Much Larger

If you buy songs from the iTunes Store, there's a little bonus: not only does it download the album art (so you can see it in the bottom-left corner of iTunes. If you don't have this feature on, just click on the fourth icon from the left beneath your Source list), but if you click directly on the album art, a separate floating window will appear with a much larger version of the cover.

Keeping an Eye on Your Spending

Although Apple knows exactly how much money you've been spending recently at the iTunes Store, you might want to know yourself (so you can prepare items that will need to be pawned). To find out how much you've spent, just click on the account button (the one that shows your ID or screen name) in the upper-right corner of the iTunes Store (if you're not already logged in, it'll say "Sign In" and when you click on it, it'll ask you for your ID and password). On your Apple Account Information page, you'll find a button called **Purchase History**. Click it and get ready to freak out as all the purchases, and their costs, are listed one after another. When you've wiped away your tears, press the Done button, because "you're done."

---

iTip: Log Out If You Leave

*If you're using the iTunes Store at work and you duck out for lunch, someone else could duck into your office, buy a few songs on your dime, download them to their iPod, and you won't know what happened until your Visa bill arrives. So, when you know you're stepping away for a few minutes, move your cursor over the account button (the one that shows your screen name) at the top right of the iTunes Store window, click on the little arrow that appears to the right of your screen name, and choose **Sign Out** from the pop-up menu. That way, no one can come in and abuse your account while you're out. When you return, just log back in and continue downloading songs on company time.*

Protect Yourself from Getting Ripped Off

If you sell your computer or give it to someone else (maybe someone else within your company will wind up using your old machine), you definitely want to "deauthorize" it first, or they may be able to buy songs from the iTunes Store, and charge them to your account. To deauthorize your computer, go under the Store menu in iTunes and choose **Deauthorize Computer**. When the dialog appears, click OK and the computer you're currently using will be deactivated. *Note:* Just erasing and reformatting a hard drive will not deauthorize a computer—you have to deauthorize it manually, as shown here.

---

iTip: Adding More Album Art

You can actually have more than one album cover per song—meaning there's an import cover, or an extended mix cover, or single cover, etc. Just select the song in iTunes, then drag the cover you want from your Web browser (from whatever webpage you found the cover on) and drop it right over the cover that's in the Artwork and Video Viewer in the bottom left of iTunes. You'll notice little arrows will appear above your album art, so you can cycle through to see the different covers.

Setting Up an iTunes Allowance

Want a high-tech way to spoil your kids? How about giving them an iTunes Store download allowance? It's scarily convenient, because once you choose how much they get each month, it's all automated from there—the iTunes Store credits their account each month and charges your credit card. It's downright eerie. Now, although I'm poking some fun at it here, when you think about it, this is much safer than giving them your (or their own) credit card, because you determine exactly how much they can spend. Here's how to set your kids up: From the iTunes Store homepage, in the list of Quick Links at the top right, click on **Buy iTunes Gifts**. On this page, click on the **Set Up an Allowance Now link** under Allowances near the bottom. This brings up the Set Up an iTunes Allowance page, where you can give your child an allowance of up to $50 a month. Once you've entered your information, click Continue. When your child signs into his account, Apple will deliver the good news.

---

iTip: iTunes Store Gift Certificates

*Another one of my favorite iTunes Store features is the ability to email or mail a friend a gift certificate for the ITS. Just go to the iTunes Store, sign in, and click on **Buy iTunes Gifts** (under Quick Links at the top right of the homepage), then choose the type of gift you want to send. Also, if someone sent you an iTunes Store gift, you can redeem it by clicking on **Redeem** under Quick Links. Once you redeem your gift, the amount of it will be displayed to the left of your screen name, and will keep a running tally as you buy stuff.*

Keeping Naughty Videos from the Kids

Okay, so you bought your 12-year-old son an iPod. Here's the thing, though: there's nothing to stop him from downloading explicit audio and video podcasts, or music with lyrics so nasty they'd make Snoop Dogg blush, or even R-rated movies. So, what's to keep your child from getting his hands on all this naughty stuff? You are. Well, you and the parental controls built into iTunes, which are designed to help you keep naughty stuff off of your kid's iPod. You do this in the iTunes Preferences (press **Command-, [comma; PC: Ctrl-,]** to bring up the dialog) by clicking on **Parental** at the top of the dialog to bring up the parental controls (shown above). Here you can choose to restrict entire sources of content (like podcasts, radio, etc.), or to restrict music downloads in the iTunes Store based on the Explicit rating tagged to adult content, or to restrict TV shows and movies based on their ratings (or even apps, if they have an iPod touch). Once you make your choices (this is important), click on the Lock icon to lock and password protect these changes, or your 12-year old will quickly disable those restrictions (never underestimate a 12-year old on a computer). Now click OK, and you gain some modicum of peace of mind.

---

iTip: Finding Your Way Back to Where You Were

If you ever get lost in the iTunes Store, either look up in the top-left corner of the main window for a clickable path showing where you are or near the bottom for buttons that do the same thing.

Telling Your Friends About Cool Albums

If you find a really cool album, you'll probably want to tell other people about it (well, at least I always do—it's a sickness). Anyway, the iTunes Store makes it easy. You can Right-click directly on the album's cover image and then choose **Copy Link** from the contextual menu (as shown here). Now head over your email application, open a new email message window, and just paste that link into your message. When your friend gets the email and clicks the link, it'll take them right to that album in the iTunes Store (provided, of course, that they have iTunes installed on their computer).

---

iTip: Finding the Latest Albums from Artists You Already Own

*If you click on the **My Alerts link** (at the bottom of the Quick Links section near the top right of the iTunes Store homepage), it takes you to a window that shows new albums released by artists you've already downloaded from the ITS. In fact, while you're there, you can sign up to get an email as soon as a new song from one of "your artists" is released (just click the **Send Me Email Notifications** link in the top-right corner). If you're waiting for a song or album to be released by an artist you haven't downloaded before, just do a search for that artist, click on their name in the search results to launch that artist's page, and then on the right side of the page, click on **Alert Me**.*

Spreading the Word on Facebook and Twitter

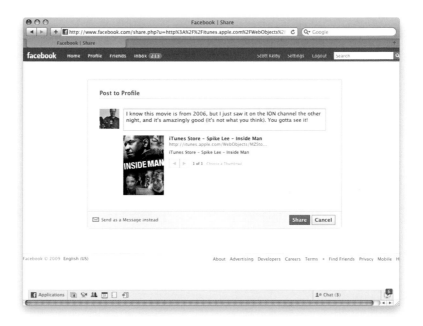

If you come across an album, TV show, or movie, and you want to tell your Facebook friends or the people who follow you on Twitter about it, you can do that right from the iTunes Store itself. Best of all, it not only sends a link to the song (or movie, TV show, etc.), it even posts cover art, as well (as seen above). Here's how it works: when you find something you want to share with your social media buddies, just click on the right side of the Buy button (on that little down-facing arrow) and choose either **Share On Facebook** or **Share On Twitter**. This launches a page like the one you see above, with the iTunes info (and link) already embedded into the page. All you have to do is type a few lines and hit Share. Pretty sweet!

---

iTip: Completing an Album

*If you've got a song or two from a particular album, you can have the iTunes Store "finish off" that album for you by automatically finding the missing songs you need to complete the album, compiling them, and letting you buy and download them all at once. Just click on the **Complete My Album link** (under Quick Links, at the top right of the homepage), and it shows all the albums that are eligible to be completed, which songs are required to complete them, and how much that would cost. Pretty handy, eh?*

Letting Other People Listen to Your Music

If you're on a network (at work, at school, etc.), you can let other people on that local network listen to your Music Library or playlists right from their copy of iTunes on their computer. The only downside is that they won't get to hear songs you bought from the iTunes Store before May 2007, because back then all the songs had DRM (Digital Rights Management) protection built in, so it just skips those songs (although you can update those songs to be DRM-free, so then they'd hear them—see page 177). To share your music, go to the iTunes Preferences **(Command-, [comma; PC: Ctrl-,])**, click on Sharing at the top of the dialog, and turn on the **Share My Library on My Local Network checkbox**. You'll then have the option to choose to share your entire Library, or just selected playlists (that way, if you have a playlist named "My Favorite Backstreet Boys Songs," you can hide it by not turning on its checkbox). Now, when someone looks under Shared in the Source list on the left side of their iTunes window, they'll see your name. To see and hear your play-lists, all they have to do is click on your name, then click on the playlist or song of yours they want to hear, and it plays right on their computer (pretty slick—I know). By the way: the people you're sharing with on your local network can only hear your songs—they can't copy them to their computer, edit your playlists, or anything like that. However, if you have a wireless network at your home, and not only want to share songs with your family, but let them be able to copy your songs onto their individual computers, then you'd use the Home Sharing feature (see the next page).

Sharing Your Stuff with Family

If you have a network set up in your home (including a Wi-Fi network), you can share your media with other household members using iTunes' Home Sharing feature, and they can also copy your media onto their own computers (not just music—we're talking movies, TV shows, apps, etc.). Here's how to set this up: In the Source list on the left side of iTunes, under Shared, click on Home Sharing (if it's not there, you can turn it on by going under the Advanced menu and choosing **Turn On Home Sharing**). It'll ask you to enter your iTunes Store account name and password (so do that), then click **Create Home Share**. Now, go to your family member's computer, launch iTunes and do the exact same thing there, but (and this is important) you must use the same account name and password on their computer that you used on yours (that's what links them together). Your name will now appear under Shared in their Source list, and when they click on it, they'll have access to all your songs, movies, podcasts—you name it. If they double-click on a song or video, they'll be able to hear/see it. If they want a copy of something in their iTunes Library, they can literally just drag-and-drop it from your shared Library to their iTunes Library. Also, they can set it up so they get a copy of any new stuff you buy from the iTunes Store automatically by clicking on your Library, then clicking on the Settings button (in the bottom-right corner of the window) to bring up a list of options where they can choose which types of content they want copies of (music, movies, TV shows, etc.), then clicking OK, and it will do the transfers for them.

Speeding Up Sharing and Previews

If you're on a local network, chances are you've got a direct and pretty speedy connection to that network. If that's the case, you can speed things up even more by tweaking an iTunes preference that will accelerate the loading of both the iTunes Store previews, and of shared playlists across your network. What you're doing is just shrinking the iTunes Streaming Buffer Size, meaning it buffers a smaller amount of info before it begins playing, so you see previews faster and hear shared songs faster. Now, if that all sounds confusing, it should. So, does it really matter what kind of magic goes into making iTunes run faster? No? Great, then do this: Go to iTunes Preferences (found under the iTunes menu on a Mac or the Edit menu on a Windows PC) and click on Advanced at the top of the dialog. From the **Streaming Buffer Size pop-up menu**, choose **Small**, click OK, and now things will move faster. See, that was fairly painless, eh, Bunky?

A Real Album Experience with iTunes LPs

When everything went digital and we stopped buying physical CDs, we did lose a nice aspect of them you'd often get as part of the CD package—all the liner notes, album art, lyrics, and other bonus stuff (like videos). Luckily, you can get a similar experience again when you buy a full album of music from the iTunes Store (but in a digital way and only in iTunes on your computer—not in the iTunes app on your iPod touch. When you purchase an album with an iTunes LP on your iPod, you'll get the iTunes LP the next time you sync your iPod with your computer). To see the albums that have iTunes LPs, on the Music homepage, click on the **iTunes LP link** under Music Quick Links at the top right. Also, you'll know if an album has an LP if, on the album's page, you see the iTunes LP icon in the top-right corner and an iTunes LP at the top of the album's song list. When you buy the entire album, the LP downloads automatically—right along with your songs—and you'll see a little stack of paper icon beside its name in your Music Library. Double-click on it, and it appears in the main window (as shown above).

Getting Movie Bonus Content (Like You Do on DVDs)

You can hardly find a movie on DVD these days that doesn't include a second disc with bonus content, which usually includes things like the director's commentaries, or the original theatrical trailer, or bios on the cast, or behind-the-scenes video, or...well...you know—the typical stuff. Anyway, that's one thing you used to have to give up when you downloaded movies from the iTunes Store, but now with some movies, you can get that bonus material downloaded right along with the movie (it's called **"iTunes Extras"**), and you can view it right within iTunes itself (unfortunately, they don't transfer over to your iPod—this is an iTunes-only feature).

---

iTip: Gift a Song, or Album, or Movie

*If you run across a song (or movie) you really, really like, you can actually buy the song, and send it to a friend as a gift (your friend will be emailed a link where they can down-load your thoughtful gift). Here's how to send a song, or an entire album (or a music video), to a friend as a gift: Go to the iTunes Store and find the page for the song, album, movie, etc., that you want to send as a gift. Then, click on the down-facing arrow to the right of the Buy button, and choose **Gift This (Media Type)**. This takes you to a page where you can choose how you'd like the gift delivered to your friend.*

Moving Your Purchases to Another Computer

If you want to transfer music or videos that you've purchased in the iTunes Store to another computer, the fastest and easiest way to do this is to move them using your iPod (by the way, this just moves your music and videos purchased from the iTunes Store, not any music you imported from CDs or any other way). Here's how it's done: Apple allows you to authorize up to five computers to move your purchased videos and music from the iTunes Store onto, and then play them. Once your purchased music (and videos) has been downloaded onto your iPod, just connect your iPod to another one of your authorized computers and a dialog will appear asking you if you want to transfer your purchased videos and music to this other authorized computer. If, for some reason, that dialog doesn't appear, just go under the File menu, choose **Transfer Purchases from iPod**, and it does the rest. By the way, if you're not sure how to authorize a computer to play your purchased music and videos, read the tip below.

---

iTip: Automatic Authorizing

Authorizing is an automatic thing: if you plug in your iPod to another one of your computers (like a laptop for instance), a dialog appears letting you know that this isn't an authorized computer, but as long as you haven't used up your five-computer limit, it will allow you to authorize that computer right there on the spot. Feel the power!

Chapter Ten

Tip Drill
Cool iTunes Tips & Tricks

You'd think "Tip Drill" for a chapter about iTunes tips is just about as perfect a name as you can come up with. It totally makes sense, plus it's the name of a song from Nelly, and it's the name of a DVD documentary (which features—and was inspired by—the Nelly song of the same name). Now, being the NFL football fan that I am (Go Bucs!), when I hear "tip drill," I think of a practice drill in which a passed ball gets "tipped" by a member of the defense, making that ball much easier to intercept. NFL teams practice these tip drills all the time, and that's why in a real game, when a pass gets tipped, everybody holds their breath, because it's probably going to be intercepted. So, when I came across a song named "Tip Drill," I was drawn to it. Now, this song is available from the iTunes Store, but when I searched on the Web for the lyrics, I learned that "Tip Drill" is a very naughty song. In fact, it's mega-naughty. If my 12-year-old ever heard this song, there wouldn't be enough soap in the world to clear out the naughty passing through his ears. I'm not sure the Explicit warning that the iTunes Store has on it is strong enough. It might just have to say "Yikes!" or "Whoa, Nelly!" (Sorry, that was lame.) So, I searched for the DVD, which (not surprisingly) is about somewhat naughty things. So, to ensure that this chapter doesn't get an NC-17 rating, let's bend our song-or-movie-title-chapter-name rule and use the NFL's definition of "tip drill" instead. Thanks for understanding.

Browse Your Music in Cover Flow View

Cover Flow is the most visual (and certainly coolest) way to browse through your iTunes Music Library (or any playlist), because it's kind of like browsing through an actual CD collection in your home or at the local record store. To enter **Cover Flow view**, click the third view icon from the left at the top right of iTunes (shown circled above), and the covers appear above your music list. You can browse through your covers in any of these three ways: (1) drag the scrubber bar directly below the covers, (2) use the Left and Right Arrow keys on your keyboard, or (3) just click on any album cover you see, even if it's partially covered, and it comes to the front. When you stop on a cover, the song info is highlighted in the list that appears below the Cover Flow view. To hear that song, either double-click on the album art itself, or on the highlighted song in the list. Also, while you're in this Cover Flow view, you can choose different sorting methods (by name, by genre, by rating, etc.) just like you would in a regular playlist view by clicking on the column headers in the list below the Cover Flow view, and the covers are then displayed in that order. Wicked cool, eh?

---

iTip: Jump to the Right Song

In Cover Flow view, if you know the name of the song you want and the Name category is highlighted in your music list, you can just type the first few letters of the song name and iTunes will jump to the first song in your playlist that begins with those letters. This also works for Artist and Album when those categories are highlighted.

Browse Your Music in Grid View

iTunes has another view—Grid view—that, like Cover Flow, shows your music by album cover. You can switch to **Grid view** by clicking the middle view icon at the top right of iTunes (circled above). When you see an album that you want to hear, just double-click on it to see the songs on the album and then just double-click on the song you want to hear to begin playing it. You can view the grid by album, artist, genre, or composer. To turn this option on, from the View menu, choose Grid View, then choose **Show Header**. This allows you to quickly get to the kind of music you want to listen to. For example, if you are in your Music Library and click on the Genres button (at the top center of the grid window), you can listen to all of your Rock, Jazz, or Holiday music without having to find it first and then create a playlist, or without creating a smart playlist.

---

iTip: Album Art View Is Still There

*If you've ever used Album Art view—large album covers along the left side of the main window, with the song info on the right—in previous versions of iTunes, you might think that Apple totally removed this view. But, it's actually still there. You just have to access it in a different way. To get to the **Album Art view**, all you have to do is click on the List View icon (the first icon at the top right of iTunes) and you'll notice a little right-facing triangle at the top of the first column on the left of the main window. When you click on this triangle, it will expose the album Artwork column. Clicking it again will hide this column.*

Making Sure All Your Songs Are Rated

Smart Playlist

☑ Match the following rule:

| Rating ⇕ | is less than ⇕ | ★ · · · · | ⊖ ⊕ ⊙ |

☐ Limit to `25` `items` ⇕ selected by `random` ⇕

☐ Match only checked items

☑ Live updating

⑦   (Cancel) (OK)

By now you know how important it is to rate your songs (especially if you want to make smart playlists, and believe me, you want to make smart playlists. You can find more about them in Chapter 8 and in the bonus chapter on the book's companion website). But you know (and I know) there are songs you haven't rated yet. Well, here's a quick way to find all your unrated songs and gather them in one place so you can rate them. Press-and-hold the **Option (PC: Alt) key** and click on the **Create a Playlist button** in the bottom-left corner of iTunes to bring up the Smart Playlist dialog. From the first pop-up menu, choose Rating; from the second menu, choose Is Less Than; in the stars field, click on the first dot to assign the ranking of one star; and then make sure the Limit To checkbox is turned off, so it will get all your unrated songs, and the Live Updating checkbox is turned on. Click OK, and iTunes will instantly assemble a playlist of nothing but your unrated songs. As soon as you rate a song in that playlist—boom—it jumps off of it. When you're done, connect your iPod, and iTunes will add your new ratings there, as well. See, that wasn't as hard as you thought it would be.

Adding Smooth Transitions Between Songs

Rather than a blank gap existing after each song, how would you like it if, when the song got near the end, it started fading out and the next song started fading in, just like they often do on the radio? iTunes can do this automatically—it's called "crossfading." You can add crossfading by going to the iTunes Preferences (under the iTunes menu on a Mac; under the Edit menu on a Windows PC) and clicking on Playback at the top. Next, near the top of the dialog, turn on the checkbox for **Crossfade Songs** (if it's not already), and you're set. If you want a faster (or slower) crossfade between songs, you can adjust that using the slider. The crossfades are measured in seconds, so for longer crossfades, drag the slider to the right. For shorter ones, drag it to the left.

---

iTip: How to Shuffle Albums

*Did you know that you can set iTunes to shuffle albums randomly? It will shuffle just the albums themselves—not the songs on the albums. If you want to turn this feature on, just go under the Controls menu, under Shuffle, and choose **By Albums**. Now when you turn Shuffle on (the second icon from the left below your Source list), it will shuffle your albums.*

Balancing the Volume Between Songs

One of the perils of having an eclectic taste in music is that all music isn't recorded at the same volume. For example, if the first song in one of your playlists is "Concerto for Piano No. 21 in C Major, K 467: 2nd Movement, Andante," and the next song following that happens to be "I'm a Dog" by Kid Rock, I have to tell you that when "I'm a Dog" comes on, the volume (and sheer mass) of that song will send you scrambling for the Volume slider. If there were only some way that piano concertos and rock-rap could share the same volume setting. Ah, but there is—it's called Sound Check, and this iTunes preference setting lets you automatically balance the volume between songs just like your iPod does. Just go to the iTunes Preferences (found under the iTunes menu on a Mac, or the Edit menu on a PC), and then click on Playback at the top. Next, turn on the **Sound Check checkbox** to turn on iTunes' automatic volume balancing. So now, when you glide from Frank Sinatra straight into Metallica, it'll be a smooth transition (at least, volumewise).

---

iTip: Keyboard Volume Adjustment

If you want to change the volume while you're playing a song, you don't have to grab the mouse and do it on your desktop—instead, you can adjust the volume right from your keyboard. To "crank up the jams," press **Command–Up Arrow (PC: Ctrl–Up Arrow)** and to turn it back down (when the cops arrive), press **Command–Down Arrow (PC: Ctrl–Down Arrow)**.

Making Your Music Sound Better

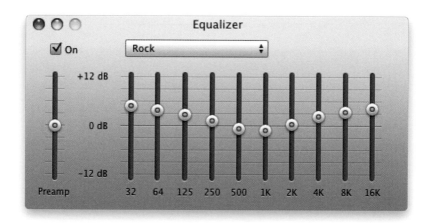

By default, the iTunes graphic equalizer (EQ) is set to flat, which is basically the same as setting the bass and treble sliders on your car stereo to the zero setting (flat is actually a good name for this state, because that's how it makes your stereo sound—flat). But you can use iTunes' built-in EQ to make your music sound dramatically better, and you don't have to understand how EQs work—presets based on the type of music you listen to are already built in. Here's how to turn on iTunes' EQ: On a Mac, go under the **Window menu** and choose **Equalizer**; on a PC, go under the **View menu** and choose **Show Equalizer**. At the top of the Equalizer dialog is a pop-up menu with presets—just choose the type of music you're listening to, and iTunes creates an EQ setting to make your music sound its best. If you want to create your own setting, just grab the sliders (bass on the left, mid-range in the middle, and highs on the right), and make your own.

---

iTip: Creating Custom EQ Presets

*If you've created your own custom EQ setting (I created one for my laptop by starting with the R&B preset and then tweaking the bass sliders), you can save it as your own custom preset. Once you've got your EQ set the way you want it, choose **Make Preset** from the presets pop-up menu in the Equalizer dialog, and name your preset in the resulting dialog. When you click OK, your preset is added to the presets pop-up menu and will appear in alphabetical order.*

Individual EQ Settings by Song

I know what you're thinking: "Okay Scott, I set my overall EQ for iTunes to Rock, but some of my songs are R&B, some are classical, and some are dance. So my rock songs will sound great, but the rest are going to be EQ'd for rock, so they won't sound their best, right?" Right. That's why iTunes lets you assign EQs to individual songs, so you can assign an R&B EQ to R&B songs, and a Classical EQ to classical pieces. Here's how: Press **Command-J (PC: Ctrl-J)** to bring up the **View Options**, then turn on the **Equalizer checkbox** and an Equalizer column will appear in your iTunes window. To assign an EQ to a song, click on the song, then click on the EQ icon, and choose the EQ you want for that song from the pop-up menu.

---

iTip: Setting the EQ for Multiple Songs

Applying EQ settings on a song-by-song basis can take some time, so here's a big timesaving shortcut: First, click on the Genre column to sort your songs by genre, then Shift-click on the first song and the last song to select all the songs in that genre. Now Right-click on any selected song, and in the contextual menu, choose **Get Info** *to bring up the Multiple Item Information dialog. Click on the Options tab, then turn on the* **Equalizer Preset checkbox,** *choose an EQ preset, and click OK.*

Editing a Song's Start/End Points

Baby Got Back

| Summary | Info | Video | Sorting | Options | Lyrics | Artwork |

Volume Adjustment: ──────────●──────────
 −100%   None   +100%

Equalizer Preset: None

Media Kind: Music

VoiceOver Language: Automatic

Rating:

☑ Start Time: 0:17

☐ Stop Time: 4:23.8

☐ Remember playback position
☐ Skip when shuffling
☐ Part of a gapless album

Previous   Next   Cancel   OK

Being able to choose when a song starts (or ends) is more important than you might think. For example, the song "Baby Got Back" by Sir Mix-A-Lot starts with two Valley girls dissing some other girl's butt. It's kind of funny the first time you hear it, but by the tenth or eleventh time, it really gets old. Luckily, iTunes lets you skip this part entirely by setting the Start Time for the song. Here's how: First, you need to find out exactly where the "good part" starts, so play the song from the beginning and note the elapsed time in the status window when the music actually starts (in "Baby Got Back" the actual music starts 17 seconds in—the girls keep talking for a few more seconds, but at least the music is playing). Now, in your Music Library (or playlist), Right-click on the song you want to edit and choose **Get Info** from the contextual menu. Click on the Options tab and you'll see checkboxes for **Start Time** and **Stop Time**. Turn on the Start Time checkbox, and then enter 0:17. That's it. Now when this song plays, it will skip over the Valley girls and get right to the music.

---

iTip: Editing the Next Song's Info

*Here are two little buttons that a lot of people miss in the Get Info dialog: the **Next and Previous buttons**. What they do is let you, without closing this dialog, edit the next (or previous) song in the current playlist or Music Library. Just click on the Next button, and the next song's info appears in this dialog, ready to edit. I know, this may not seem like the biggest deal right now, but try it a few times and you'll be surprised at how much time you'll save.*

How Many Playlists Does a Song Appear In?

If you seem to be hearing a particular song an awful lot, it may be that the song appears in several different playlists, so you wind up changing playlists but still hearing that song again. Luckily, there's a slick way to find out exactly how many (and which) playlists a particular song appears in—just Right-click on a song, and from the contextual menu that appears, go under **Show in Playlist** to see a list of the playlists that contain that song. If you see quite a long list, you'll know why you've been hearing it so much.

---

iTip: Finding Duplicates

*Because you'll wind up having hundreds, maybe thousands, of songs in iTunes, and lots of different playlists, you'll be amazed at how easy it is to have more than one copy of a song (maybe with a slightly different name, or just in different playlists, or different versions of the same song). Luckily, there's a quick way to get rid of the duplicates—just go under the File menu and choose **Show Duplicates**. This will bring up a list of all your duplicate songs. Then, if you have two (or more) copies, you can quickly click on the one(s) you want to delete and press the Delete (PC: Backspace) key on your keyboard. To go back to your Music Library or playlist, just choose Show All from the File menu.*

Moving Playlists Between Computers

If you have more than one computer (let's say you have a desktop machine and a laptop), you probably want access to your iTunes playlists on both machines, right? Well, you could set up a wireless network, blah, blah, blah, or you could simply export your playlist from your desktop machine, and then import that playlist in iTunes on your laptop. Here's how: Just Right-click on the playlist you want to export, and choose **Export** from the contextual menu that appears. Now, save it and transfer that playlist (text file) to your other computer (put it on a USB drive, burn it to CD, email it to yourself, whatever), then go under the iTunes File menu and choose **Import Playlist** from the Library submenu. Locate that exported playlist file, click Open, and that playlist is now in your laptop's iTunes. Ahhh, but there's a catch (you knew it couldn't be that easy, right?). What you've imported is a "list" of songs—not the songs themselves. If the songs don't already appear in the iTunes Music Library on the "other" computer, you may need to transfer the actual MP3 and AAC song files (again, you can burn them to CD or use your iPod as a hard drive [see Chapter 3 for how to do that]). Once the songs are copied onto your laptop (and imported into your iTunes Music Library), you can then use your imported playlist to hear those songs.

Finding Your Originals for Easy Backup

Backing up your songs is important just in case anything ever happens to your hard disk, but if you haven't consolidated all your songs into the iTunes folder (as shown in Chapter 7), finding all your original songs to back up might be quite a chore. Well, here's something that can make your life a little easier: To find a song's original location on your hard disk, just Right-click on the song in your playlist or Music Library, then from the contextual menu that appears, choose **Show in Finder** on your Mac or **Show in Windows Explorer** on your PC. The folder where the song is located will appear in the foreground, making it easy to copy to a backup disk.

---

iTip: Changing the Font Size

*The default size for some type in iTunes is fairly small, and that's cool if you're 15, but if you're older (like 18 or 19), you might want the font size a bit bigger. You can do that by going to iTunes' Preferences (on a Mac, it's under the iTunes menu; on a Windows PC, it's under the Edit menu) and clicking on General up top. You'll see pop-up menus in the dialog for **Source Text** (the menus and such) and **List Text** (the text you see in your playlists and Library). Just make sure Large is selected in both pop-up menus to make the font size larger.*

Printing Your Own CD Jewel Case Inserts

Print "R&B"

Print: ● CD jewel case insert
○ Song listing
○ Album listing

Theme: Mosaic ⬍

Prints a collage of available album artwork from the songs in your selected playlist or library. The back also features the album artwork. Prints in full color.

(Page Setup...)   (Cancel) (Print...)

If you've burned one of your playlists to CD, you can also have iTunes print out a CD jewel case insert for you, making it easy to keep track of what's on each CD you've burned. Start by choosing the playlist you just burned to CD by clicking on it in the Source list on the left side of iTunes. Then go under the File menu and choose **Print**. When the Print dialog appears, click on the **Print: CD Jewel Case Insert radio button** (if it's not already selected). iTunes will automatically compile a list of the songs in that playlist, along with their running times, and you even have a pop-up menu where you can choose from a selection of professional-looking "themes" for your insert, including ones that include either multiple or single album covers (you'll see a preview of it on the right side of the dialog). Once you choose your theme, just click the Print button, choose your paper size or printer in the resulting dialog, and wait for your way-cool jewel case insert to spit out of the printer.

---

iTip: The Ultimate Onscreen Space Saver

*For a space-saving version of iTunes, just click on the **green + (plus sign) button** in the upper-left corner of iTunes (on a Mac), which shrinks it into the Mini Player (on a Windows PC, choose **Switch to Mini Player** from the View menu, or press **Ctrl-M**). Also, since it's so small, you can have it always appear in front of your other open applications. Go to iTunes' Preferences, click on Advanced up top, turn on the check-box for **Keep Mini Player on Top of All Other Windows**, and then click OK.*

Printing Song and Album Listings

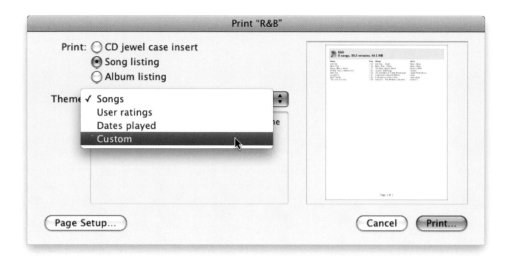

Besides printing CD jewel case inserts, iTunes also lets you print complete lists of songs, albums, or your entire iTunes Music Library (these are great to have on hand in case your computer is ever lost, stolen, or just dies a horrible, grisly death). Besides just printing simple lists, you also have control over how much information is displayed in these lists. For simple playlists, you can decide if you want title, artist, album name, running time, etc., or you can choose a layout that includes your personal ratings. You can have the list include the last date you played each song, or you can get a complete printout of the iTunes window view—it's all up to you. Just make your choice from the Theme pop-up menu that appears when you choose **Print** from the File menu, and then click on the **Song Listing radio button**. If you want a printout of all your albums, click on the **Album Listing radio button** instead, and you'll get both the album cover (if your songs have one) and a listing of which songs from that album appear in your playlist.

---

iTip: How to Delete Album Art

If you have album art along with one of your songs, and you decide you want to delete that art, Right-click on the song, and from the contextual menu that appears, choose **Get Info**. *When the dialog appears, click on the Artwork tab at the top, then click on your artwork in the preview window and the* **Delete button** *below it will activate. Click it, and it's gone!*

---

iTunes Radio Is on the Air!

If you've got an Internet connection, there's another side to iTunes that they don't talk about at parties, and that's iTunes Radio. Well, it's not exactly FM radio, but instead it's a list of hundreds of streaming Internet radio stations, broadcasting everything from reggae to talk shows, from metal to classical (and everything in between). The reason many people don't know about this cool hidden feature is that it's likely hidden from view in the Source list. To see the current list of stations, go to the iTunes Preferences (on a Mac, it's under the iTunes menu; on a Windows PC, it's under the Edit menu) and click on General up top. Then, in the Show section, turn on the checkbox for **Radio** and click OK. Now a Radio link will appear in your Source list under Library. Click on it to see the list of radio genres. To see the stations currently broadcasting for a particular genre, double-click the genre's name. To listen to a station, just double-click the station's name in the list. Also, to see the name and artist for the current song, look up in the iTunes status window.

---

iTip: Making a Playlist of Your Favorite Radio Stations

*Put your favorite radio stations into a playlist as if they were songs by clicking the **Create a Playlist button** in the bottom-left corner of iTunes, naming your playlist "Radio," then clicking on the Radio link in the Source list. Find the stations you like, and drag-and-drop them right into your Radio playlist.*

It's Time to Get Visual

If you ever wanted a glimpse of what your parents' lives were like back when they were in their 20s, just press **Command-T (PC: Ctrl-T)**, which turns on iTunes' visual effects (called the **"Visualizer"**). So why did Apple include these "way out" (a '60s term) visuals in iTunes? So your parents could relate and feel good about buying you a computer and an iPod (hey, it's possible). Anyway, the images created by the Visualizer are actually pretty cool because they react to the music you're playing in iTunes, and just watching them gives you the munchies (did I say that out loud?). *Warning:* Whatever you do, don't buy the single "Are You Experienced?" by Jimi Hendrix (from the iTunes Store) and have it playing while running the Visualizer as your parents walk by your screen. They'll totally freak (and may quit their jobs).

---

iTip: Full-Screen Visualizing

*Normally, the Visualizer "does its thing" by taking over your iTunes window, but we need to experience the entire trip in its full-screen splendor. So start the Visualizer (seen above), press **Command-F (PC: Ctrl-F)**, and then sit back and stare directly into the screen. Enter into a hypnotic trance, then you can call in sick for work: "Sorry man, I can't come in today. I'm hypnotized." By the way, to end your full-screen "trance," press the **Esc key** on your keyboard. To switch back from Full Screen to containing the Visualizer within the iTunes window, press Command-F again.*

Extreme Visuals

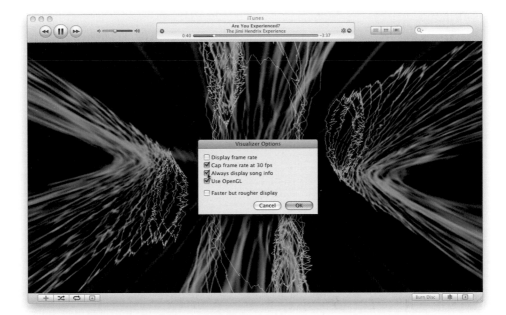

When the Visualizer is running and a new song starts, the song's name, artist, album art (if present), and album name appear for a few moments in the bottom-left corner of the screen, then they slowly fade away (so as not to distract from the mind-bending array of patterns that will soon take over your screen, and perhaps even your life). However, if you're using the Classic Visualizer, and you'd like the song info not to fade away—to always be displayed—just go under the View menu, under Visualizer, choose Options, and turn on the checkbox for **Always Display Song Info**. Plus, if the song you're playing has accompanying album art, it's displayed, too. And while you're in the Visualizer menu, you can also choose the SoftSkies, Lathe, Jelly, or Stix options (on those faster machines). Try 'em out—mesmerizing! (These features may vary depending on your computer and iTunes version.)

---

iTip: Controlling the Visuals

*If you think the Visualizer is just a random set of visual randomness that's totally random, well, my friend, I have a startling revelation for you—it only "kind of" is. That's because you actually can control some aspects of the Visualizer while it's...well...visualizing. To see the **Help options** onscreen, just press the **Question Mark (?) key** on your keyboard. You'll see that there are different one-key commands you can press while the Visualizer is running to make it bend to your every whim. So what are these one-key wonders? Just select an option and press the corresponding key on your keyboard to see.*

Chapter Eleven
Lido Shuffle
Using Your iPod shuffle

When I heard Apple chose to name their flash-memory-based iPod the "iPod shuffle," I was thrilled—mostly because it made my job of coming up with a song-based title for this chapter much easier. Two songs immediately came to mind: I could've gone with Queen's "Flash," and in most any situation, going with a Queen song is a safe bet, as they're rather revered in the rock music world. However, the song "Flash" sucks. I'm sorry, but it does. You know it does. I know it does. If I played the song for my 12-year-old son (who thankfully doesn't use the word "sucks"), even he would find himself with no other choice but to use the word "sucks," as well, and I don't want to put him in that awkward position. So, instead, I went with "Lido Shuffle," which is one of Boz Skaggs' coolest songs. Now, both of these songs are from the '80s, which automatically means they come with a measure of suckiness built right in, but we're simply going to overlook that, because it makes my job of naming the chapter even easier, and really, that's what this is all about: making my life easy. Hey, speaking of easy (how's that for a lame segue?), the iPod shuffle is fairly easy, thanks to the fact that it has no screen. When I first learned it had no screen, rather than calling it the iPod shuffle, I thought Apple should've named it something like iPod Blind or iPod in the Dark. Sadly, Apple never called me for my opinion. Or, I would've told them to name it iPod Bad Queen Song. That's probably why Apple didn't call.

Automatically Getting Songs onto Your iPod shuffle

To get songs onto your iPod shuffle, connect it to your computer, and by default iTunes will try to copy all your iTunes music onto it. If you've got a 2-GB shuffle, it'll hold around 500 songs; if you've got the 4-GB model, it'll hold around 1,000 songs. If you have more songs in iTunes than that, you'll get a warning that you've got too many, so you can either: (a) choose to have it fill your shuffle with as many random songs from your Music Library as possible until it's full, or (b) choose which playlists get copied over onto your shuffle. You do this by clicking on your iPod shuffle (under Devices in the Source list on the left side of iTunes), then clicking on the Music tab at the top of the main window. With the **Sync Music checkbox** turned on, if you can fit your entire Music Library on your shuffle, you can just go ahead and choose **Entire Music Library**. If you have more songs than your shuffle will hold, instead choose **Selected Playlists, Artists, and Genres** (as shown above), then turn on the checkboxes beside the playlists, artists, or genres you want copied over to your shuffle, and click the Apply button. If you look at the bottom of the iTunes window, you'll see how much space you have left on your shuffle as songs are being loaded.

---

iTip: Deleting a Song

*To delete a song from your iPod shuffle, first connect it to your computer, then under the Devices list on the left side of iTunes, click on Music beneath your shuffle and all the songs on your shuffle will appear in the main window. To delete a song, just click on it and press the **Delete (PC: Backspace) key** on your keyboard.*

Manually Adding Songs to Your iPod shuffle

You don't have to automatically sync to get songs onto your iPod shuffle. When you have your shuffle connected to your computer, click on it under Devices in the Source list (on the left side of iTunes), and on the Summary tab, turn on the **Manually Manage Music checkbox**. Click on your iTunes Music Library and you can now just drag-and-drop the songs that you want from your Music Library directly onto your shuffle icon in the Source list and they'll be added to your shuffle's Music Library. You can also automatically add songs to your shuffle, while still manually managing your music, by using **Autofill**. Just click on Music beneath your shuffle in the Source list and, from the Autofill From pop-up menu at the bottom of the main window, choose your entire Music Library or just a play-list. Click Autofill and your selected music will be copied to your shuffle. (*Note:* Click on the Settings button in the Autofill section for options on how Autofill will fill your shuffle.)

---

iTip: More Ways to Get Music onto Your iPod shuffle

*If you choose to sync only selected playlists, artists, and genres (see the previous page), but you still have space left on your shuffle, turn on the **Automatically Fill Free Space with Songs checkbox**, and iTunes will randomly add more songs from your Music Library until your shuffle is full. If you want to choose individual songs, rather than playlists, etc., on the Summary tab, turn on the **Sync Only Checked Songs checkbox**. Then, go in your Music Library, and turn off the checkboxes for any songs you don't want copied to your shuffle.*

The Stuff on Top of Your iPod shuffle

On the top of your iPod shuffle is a three-way switch—this is your on/off switch. Just slide the round chrome button over one notch (to the center) to turn the shuffle on and set it so your songs play in order (you'll see a green bar appear behind the left side of that round switch, and the little green LED status light will come on for just a few seconds to let you know it's turned on). If you slide the switch over another notch (so the little LED light turns yellow), that sets it to Shuffle mode, so the songs will now play in a random order. By the way, when you're done listening to your shuffle, make sure you turn it back off, or the battery will run down. Lastly, the little hole on top is where you plug in your earphones (I know—that was kinda obvious, eh?).

---

iTip: If Your shuffle Starts Acting Weird, Reset It

If your iPod shuffle won't play songs, you may just need to reset it. Turn it off by sliding the round three-way switch on the top of the shuffle to the Off position (you won't see any green), and leave it off for 10 seconds. Then turn it back on, and that should do the trick.

Playing Music on Your iPod shuffle

The controls for your iPod shuffle are found on that thin little white bar attached to the right earphone cord—right up near the earphone itself. To play or pause a song, just click the flat Center button once on that thin little bar. To jump to the next song, double-click the Center button, and to play the previous song again, click it three times. To jump back to the beginning of your playlist, just click the Center button three times really fast and then click-and-hold it. To hear the name and artist of the currently playing song, click-and-hold the Center button and VoiceOver (see page 217) will tell you. To change to a different playlist, click-and-hold the Center button until you hear a tone, then again using Voice-Over, it will tell you the name of each playlist you've copied over to your shuffle. Just click the Center button when it comes to the one you want. To turn the volume up, click the + (plus sign) button, and to lower it, click the − (minus sign) button. That's pretty much it.

---

iTip: Listening to Audiobooks and Podcasts

*To sync audiobooks along with your music, on the Music tab, choose **Selected Playlists, Artists, and Genres**, and turn on the **Audiobooks checkbox** in the Playlists section (or you can just drag-and-drop them from your iTunes Audiobooks Library onto your iPod). To get podcasts onto your iPod shuffle, on the Podcasts tab, turn on the **Sync Podcasts checkbox**, make your podcast selections, and click Apply.*

Checking Your Battery Life

The little LED light on the top of your iPod shuffle shows you how much battery life is left, and there are three ways to check it: (1) If you turn the shuffle off and right back on, the LED gives you a battery reading—if it's green, you have a decent charge (at least 50%); if the LED appears yellow, your battery is getting low; and if it's red, it's just about dead (in other words, it's time to recharge). If no LED light comes on at all, it's a little brick—the battery's dead and you need to plug it into your computer (using the USB cable that came with your shuffle) for at least two hours for a decent charge (or about three hours for a full charge). (2) When you have the earphones connected (and VoiceOver enabled—see the next page), you can have your shuffle actually verbally tell you the battery status (even while you have music playing)—just turn your shuffle off and quickly right back on, and through the earphones, it will literally tell you the approximate percentage of charge (50%, 75%, etc. But, be sure to be quick about it. Turn it off, then back on, *quickly*. If you have music playing and it stops, you're not doing it quickly enough). Lastly, (3) if your shuffle is connected to your computer (and your shuffle is turned on), you'll see the LED slowly flashing, which just means it's charging. When the charge is complete, it'll turn solid green.

Getting Your shuffle to Talk to You

To have your iPod shuffle give you voice feedback (everything from the name and artist of the currently playing song, to how much battery charge you have left), you start by connecting your shuffle to your computer, then clicking on it under Devices in the Source list on the left side of iTunes. On the Summary tab, under Voice Feedback, turn on the **Enable VoiceOver checkbox** (as shown above). Now click the Apply button (in the bottom-right corner of the window), and it will download the VoiceOver kit to your iPod shuffle (it takes a few minutes to download).

---

iTip: Finding the Serial Number

Want to know where the serial number for your iPod shuffle is located? If you open the iPod shuffle's clip, you'll see two rectangular bars—one mounted on the unit itself, and one on the clip. The serial number is written right above the bar on the body of the unit.

Storing Other Files on Your iPod shuffle

Besides storing music, you can configure your iPod shuffle to hold non-audio files, as well, so it can double as a flash drive. Here's how: Connect your shuffle to your computer, and in the Source list on the left side of iTunes, under Devices, click on it, then click on the Summary tab at the top of the main window. In the Options section, turn on the **Enable Disk Use checkbox**. Click Apply and your iPod shuffle will appear on your desktop on a Mac or as an available drive on a Windows PC. Now just drag-and-drop any type of file right onto it, like it's a portable flash drive. *Note:* To protect the data on your shuffle, always click on the Eject button in iTunes (to the right of it in the Source list) before you disconnect it when you've turned on Enable Disk Use or you're manually managing music. Otherwise, you can just disconnect it anytime it's not syncing with iTunes (it will say "OK to disconnect" at the top of the iTunes window).

---

iTip: Fitting More Songs on Your iPod shuffle

*If you want to fit as many songs on your iPod shuffle as possible, you can have iTunes automatically convert your MP3, AIFF, and WAV files to AAC format. Click on your iPod shuffle in the Source list, then click on the Summary tab in the main window, scroll down to Options, and turn on the checkbox for **Convert Higher Bit Rate Songs to 128 kbps AAC**. Oh yeah, you don't have to worry about altering your original songs—it only converts songs as they're copied onto your iPod shuffle; the songs in your iTunes Music Library remain untouched.*

Index

A

AAC format, 25, 146, 218
Account Information page, 180
Address Book, 48, 113
alarm function, 34, 130
album art
  browsing, 22, 90, 194–195
  Cover Flow view, 22, 90, 194
  deleting, 206
  downloading, 179, 181
  Grid view, 195
  large version of, 179
  substitutes for, 82
Album Art view, 195
albums
  buying, 175
  completing, 185
  gapless playback of, 149
  giving as gifts, 190
  On-The-Go playlists and, 27
  printing lists of, 206
  seeing songs on, 84
  shuffle feature for, 197
alerts feature, 184
allowance, iTunes, 182
apps, 99–101
  deleting, 100
  downloading, 99
  force quitting, 131
  rearranging on iPod touch, 80
  updates/bug fixes, 101
artists
  ITS Alert feature, 184
  playing all songs by, 84
  playlists based on, 27
audio podcasts, 94
audiobooks, 33, 89, 215
authorizing computers, 61, 191
auto-complete feature, 102
Autofill option, 213
auto-import feature, 146
auto-naming feature, 147
AV Cable connection, 59, 73, 98

B

backing up files, 179, 204
Backlight, 14
battery, 2, 17
battery life
  Backlight and, 14
  Brightness slider and, 61
  status indicators for, 16, 216
  videos and, 61
bookmarks, 108, 109, 124
Brightness slider, 15, 61
Burn Disc button, 144, 145
Burn Settings dialog, 145

burning CDs, 144–145
business presentations, 74

C

calculator, 126
calendars, 48, 112
Camera Roll, 62
CDs, 144–147
Celebrity Playlists feature, 173
Center button, 10, 47
Cinematic video mode, 95
Click Wheel, 10, 11
Clicker settings, 28
clock features, 29, 34, 130
columns
  hiding/showing in iTunes, 138
  rearranging in playlists, 156
.com button, 106
computers
  authorizing/deauthorizing, 61, 191
  locating music files on, 204
  transferring media between, 61, 191, 203
consolidating music, 151
contacts, 48, 113, 120
copy-and-paste function, 104
Cover Flow view, 22, 90, 194
crossfading songs, 197

D

Date & Time menu, 29
deauthorizing computers, 181
Digital Rights Management (DRM), 177, 186
Directions screen, 121, 122
Dock, 8, 59
downloads, 178
driving directions, 121, 122
Drop Pin feature, 122
duplicate songs, 202

E

editing song info, 140, 201
Eject icon, 2, 8, 218
email features (iPod touch), 114–117
Enable Disk Use feature, 44, 74, 218
Equalizer (EQ) feature, 29, 199–200
error correction, 145
explicit lyrics, 153

F

Facebook, 185
family sharing, 187
Fast-Forward button, 10, 11, 82
file formats
  music, 25, 146, 218

video, 59
finding. *See* Search function
Fitness settings, 39
FM radio (iPod nano), 37–38
  listening to, 37
  pausing live, 38
folders
  importing photos from, 68, 69
  playlist, 161
force quitting apps, 131
free space info, 31

G

games, 35, 134
gaps between songs, 144, 149
Genius mixes, 88, 164
Genius playlists
  creating in iTunes, 162
  ITS recommendations, 163
  making on iPods, 28, 87
Genius Sidebar, 163
genres
  browsing ITS by, 172
  creating custom, 147
  EQ settings and, 200
  playlists based on, 142, 154
Get Info dialog, 60, 140, 141, 147, 201
gift cards/certificates, 90, 182
Google search, 107
Gracenote Database, 147
Grid view, 195

H

H.264 video format, 59
hard disks
  importing songs from, 5
  iPods as removable, 44, 218
  locating song files on, 204
  organizing songs on, 151
  saving space on, 146
Hold switch, 13, 46, 47
Home Sharing feature, 187

I

iMixes, 173
Import CD button, 4
importing, automatic, 146
Internet
  iPod touch access to, 105
  iTunes Radio via, 207
  See also Web features
iPhoto, 64, 68, 71
iPod
  battery indicator, 16
  charging, 2, 110
  computer connection, 2
  copying media to, 8, 57
  disconnecting, 5

iPod *(continued)*
free space info, 31, 150
hard disk mode, 44
manually updating, 45
naming/renaming, 32
resetting, 47
Screen Lock feature, 49
syncing with iTunes, 8, 9
transferring purchases from, 191
troubleshooting, 46–47
iPod classic
audiobooks on, 33
Backlight settings, 14
Brightness slider, 15
buttons/controls, 10
Cover Flow view, 22
free space info, 31
games played on, 35
Genius playlists, 28
lyrics viewed on, 141
Main Menu, 20
On-The-Go playlists, 27
pausing songs on, 10
playing songs on, 11
rating songs on, 26
Search feature, 21
shuffling songs on, 23
sleep mode, 13
Sound Check feature, 30
Stopwatch feature, 22
turning on/off, 2
videos on, 12
iPod nano
audiobooks on, 33
Backlight settings, 14
Brightness slider, 15
buttons/controls, 10
Cover Flow view, 22
FM radio, 37–38
free space info, 31
games played on, 35
Genius playlists, 28
lyrics viewed on, 141
Main Menu, 20
On-The-Go playlists, 27
pausing songs on, 10
pedometer, 39
playing songs on, 11
rating songs on, 26
recording voice memos on, 36
Search feature, 21
shooting video on, 62, 63
shuffling songs on, 23, 24
sleep mode, 13
Sound Check feature, 30
Stopwatch feature, 22
turning on/off, 2
videos on, 12
VoiceOver feature, 40

iPod shuffle, 211–218
Autofill option, 213
battery check on, 216
charging, 216
controls for, 214, 215
deleting songs from, 212
ejecting, 218
fitting more songs on, 218
getting songs into, 212–213
manually adding songs to, 213
podcasts on, 215
resetting, 214
serial number for, 217
Shuffle mode on, 214
storing files on, 218
turning on/off, 214
VoiceOver feature, 215, 217
iPod touch, 77–135
alarm feature, 130
album art on, 82, 90
apps for, 99–101
audiobooks on, 89
Bluetooth headset for, 134
calculator, 126
calendar program, 112
charging without syncing, 110
clock features, 130
contact management, 113
copying-and-pasting with, 104
Cover Flow view, 90
Delete button, 96
downloading apps for, 99
email features, 114–117
Genius mixes, 88
Genius playlists, 87
Home screen, 79–81
keyboard, 102–103
lyrics viewed on, 141
Maps app, 119–124
Music app buttons, 92
Notes app, 128
onscreen controls for, 91
On-The-Go playlists, 86
parental controls on, 96
photo features, 117–118
playing songs on, 82
playlists on, 85–87
podcast downloads to, 94
rearranging icons on, 80
redeeming gift cards from, 90
renting movies from, 97
Repeat icon, 83
scrubby slider, 83
seeing songs on albums on, 84
shuffling songs on, 24, 83
sleep timer feature, 129
Sleep/Wake button, 78, 131
slide shows on, 117
startup wallpaper, 118
stock quotes on, 127

Stopwatch feature, 131
turning on/off, 78
TV connection, 98
video modes on, 95
Voice Control for, 132
Voice Memos app, 133
volume controls, 78, 91
watching videos on, 95, 111
Weather app, 125
Web features, 105–111
Wi-Fi connections, 93
YouTube videos, 111
zooming in/out, 118
iResQ.com, 17
ITS. *See* iTunes Store
iTunes, 3, 137–151
album art in, 194–195
audio formats in, 146
auto-import feature, 146
burning CDs in, 144–145
combining tracks in, 148
converting videos in, 58
Cover Flow view, 194
crossfading songs in, 197
customizing, 138
deleting songs in, 143
downloading, 3
editing song info in, 140, 201
enlarging type size in, 204
Equalizer (EQ) feature, 199–200
finding songs in, 139
free space info in, 31, 150
gapless playback in, 149
Genius feature, 28, 162–164
genre creation in, 147
Grid view, 195
hiding/showing columns in, 138
Home Sharing feature, 187
importing songs into, 4, 5, 146
instant playlists in, 142
Internet radio via, 207
LP feature for, 189
lyrics for songs in, 141
Mini Player version of, 205
movie extras viewed in, 190
naming songs imported into, 147
organizing songs in, 151
parental controls in, 183
playlist creation in, 7
preventing syncing with, 110
rating songs in, 26, 158
resetting song play count in, 144
salvaging damaged CDs in, 145
sharing music from, 186, 187
shortcuts to ITS from, 175
song playing in, 142
sort order changes in, 149
Sound Check feature, 198
status window, 150
transferring songs from, 8

videos played in, 55, 64
viewing song info in, 138
Visualizer, 208–209
iTunes DJ, 165, 166
iTunes Extras, 190
iTunes Plus, 177
iTunes Radio, 207
iTunes Store (ITS), 3, 169–191
    account info, 100, 180
    album art downloads, 179, 181
    alerts feature, 184
    allowance feature, 182
    app downloads, 99
    audiobook downloads, 33
    authorized computers and,
        61, 181, 191
    backing up songs from, 179
    buying songs from, 176
    clickable links in, 172
    completing albums from, 185
    emailing music links from, 184
    game downloads, 35
    genre browsing in, 172
    gift certificates for, 182
    Gift This Media feature, 190
    iMix feature, 173
    international versions of, 175
    iPod touch access to, 93
    iTunes Plus link, 177
    keyboard shortcuts, 170
    logging out from, 180
    LPs available from, 189
    movies, 54, 190
    music video downloads, 54
    navigating, 170, 183
    parental controls, 183
    podcasts in, 60, 94
    Power Search feature, 174
    purchase history, 180
    request form for, 174
    searching in, 56, 171
    sharing music from, 184, 185
    shortcuts from iTunes to, 175
    song downloads, 6
    speeding up previews in, 188
    transferring purchases, 61, 191
    TV show downloads, 55
    Wish List, 176
iTunes Tagging, 38

J

jewel case inserts, 205
joining tracks, 148

L

Last Played option, 160
List View option, 195
live updating, 159
Locate Me button, 119, 123
Lock icon, 183

lock up problems, 47
LP albums, 189
lyrics
    embedding, 141
    explicit, 153

M

M4A/M4B formats, 25
Magnifying Glass icon, 139
Mail icon, 114, 115
    See also email features
Main Menu, 20
Maps app (iPod touch), 119–124
    bookmarks in, 124
    contacts located with, 120
    driving directions, 121, 122
    Drop Pin feature, 122
    finding addresses with, 119
    Locate Me button, 119, 123
    Satellite view, 123
    traffic conditions, 123
Menu button, 10, 20, 47
Mini Player, 205
mixes
    Genius, 88, 164
    party DJ, 165–166
    See also playlists
movies. *See* videos
Movies Library, 60
MP3 format, 25, 146
MPEG-4 video format, 59
multiplayer games, 134
music
    backing up, 179, 204
    browsing, 142
    buying from ITS, 176
    consolidating, 151
    converting, 218
    crossfading, 197
    deleting, 32, 143, 212
    downloading from ITS, 6, 178
    editing info for, 140, 201
    emailing links to, 184
    EQ settings for, 200
    file formats for, 25, 146
    finding, 21, 139
    genres for, 147
    giving as gifts, 190
    importing, 4, 5, 146
    joining tracks of, 148
    locating on hard disks, 204
    lyrics added to, 141
    naming automatically, 147
    pausing, 10
    playing, 11, 82
    printing lists of, 206
    rating, 26, 158, 196
    repeating, 25, 83
    request form for, 174
    resetting play count for, 144

scrubbing through, 11, 83
searching for, 21, 139
sharing over networks, 186
shuffling order of, 23, 83
skipping, 141
slide show, 71
sorting, 149, 154
start/end points for, 201
transitions between, 197
Music app, 91, 92
music videos, 54, 56, 60

N

naming/renaming
    automatic, 147
    iPods, 32
    sorting and, 156
narration speed control, 33
networks
    accessing Wi-Fi, 105
    sharing music over, 186
Nike + iPod Sport Kit, 39, 135
Notes app, 128
Now Playing info, 142

O

online forms, 110
On-The-Go playlists, 27, 86
Organize Library option, 151

P

parental controls, 96, 183
party DJ feature, 165, 166
passcode for Screen Lock, 49
Pause button, 10, 13
pedometer (iPod nano), 39
peer-to-peer gaming, 134
photo features, 67–74
    emailing photos, 117
    importing photos, 68–69
    on iPod touch, 117–118
    loading photos, 74
    slide shows, 71–73, 117
    startup wallpaper, 118
    viewing imported photos, 70
    zooming photos, 118
Play/Pause button, 2, 10, 11, 82
playlists, 153–166
    album, 27
    artist, 27
    burning, 144
    celebrity, 173
    column order in, 156
    combining, 157
    creating, 7, 161
    deleting, 155
    duplicate songs in, 202
    Genius, 28, 87, 162–164
    genres used for, 142, 154
    iMix, 173

playlists *(continued)*
instant, 142
iPod-only, 50
lists of, 157
On-The-Go, 27, 86
organizing in folders, 161
party DJ, 165–166
printing, 157
radio station, 207
rated songs and, 158
removing songs from, 143, 155
repeating, 25, 83
selected songs, 161
sharing over networks, 186
shuffling songs in, 23, 85
skipping songs in, 141, 155
smart, 158–160, 162
sorting songs in, 154
video, 12
viewing, 85
podcasts, 60, 94, 215
power on problems, 46
Power Search feature, 174
Preferences, 150
presentations, 74
previews, music, 188
printing
CD jewel case inserts, 205
playlists, 157
song/album listings, 206

Q

QuickTime application, 58
QuickTime file format, 141

R

radio
iPod nano, 37–38
iTunes, 207
rating songs, 26, 158, 196
Recents button, 124
recording voice memos, 36, 133
remote controls, 74
renting movies, 54, 97
repeating songs/playlists, 25, 83
Reset Play Count option, 144
resetting iPods, 47, 214
Rewind button, 10, 11, 82

S

Safari Web browser, 106
salvaging damaged CDs, 145
screen
Backlight, 14
Brightness slider, 15, 61
locking/unlocking, 49
scrubbing
songs, 11, 83
videos, 12, 95
search engines, 107

Search function
iPod nano/classic, 21
iPod touch, 89
ITS, 56, 171
iTunes, 139
YouTube, 111
Shake-to-Shuffle feature, 24
sharing music, 184, 185, 186, 187
short songs playlist, 160
Show in Playlist option, 202
Shuffle feature, 23
album shuffling, 197
iPod classic, 23
iPod nano, 23, 24
iPod shuffle, 214
iPod touch, 83, 85
photo shuffling, 72
playlist shuffling, 23, 85
simultaneous downloads, 178
skipping songs, 141, 155
sleep mode, 13, 78
sleep timer feature, 129
Sleep/Wake button, 78, 131
slide shows, 71–73
customizing, 72
on iPod touch, 117
music added to, 71
playing/pausing, 71
remote control of, 74
showing on TVs, 72, 73
smart playlists, 158–160
criteria options for, 159
rated songs and, 158
regular playlists from, 162
unrated songs and, 196
songs. *See* music
sorting songs, 149, 154, 156
Sound Check feature, 30, 198
special effects for videos, 63
Spotlight search feature, 89
Start/Stop Time options, 201
status window, 150
stock quotes, 127
Stopwatch feature, 22, 131
Streaming Buffer Size, 188
syncing
calendars, 48, 112
contacts, 48, 113
iPods with iTunes, 8, 9
movies, 57, 97

T

tagging songs, 38
television. *See* TV
time display, 29
time zones, 34
tracks, combining, 148
troubleshooting iPods, 46–47, 214
TV
connecting iPod touch, 98

displaying slide shows on, 72, 73
watching iPod videos on, 59
TV shows
downloading from ITS, 55
finding in ITS, 56
playing on iPods, 12

U

USB 2 cable, 2, 8

V

Video Camera, 62, 63
video podcasts, 60, 94
videos, 53–64
buying from ITS, 54
classifying, 60
converting, 58
copying to iPods, 57
deleting, 62, 96
effects added to, 63
extra content with, 190
file formats for, 59
finding in ITS, 56
home movies, 58
importing, 58, 59, 60
manually managing, 57
music videos, 54, 60
outputting to TVs, 59
playing in iTunes, 55, 64
playing on iPods, 12, 95
playlists for, 12
purchasing from ITS, 54
renting from ITS, 54, 97
scrubbing, 12, 95
transferring to computers, 64
Videos menu, 12
View Options dialog, 138
Visualizer, 208–209
Voice Control feature, 132
voice memos, 36, 133
VoiceOver feature, 40, 215, 217
volume control
iPod touch, 78, 91
keyboard shortcuts for, 198
Sound Check feature, 30, 198

W

WAV files, 141
Web features (iPod touch), 105–111
Wi-Fi connections, 93, 105
wireless headset, 134
wireless remote, 59, 74
Wish List, 176

Y

YouTube videos, 111

Z

zooming photos, 118

What's better than *Layers* magazine?
Layers magazine FREE!

Yes, you read that right. Check it …